BRIAN R. SPISAK

COMPUTATIONAL LEADERSHIP

Connecting Behavioral Science and Technology to
Optimize Decision-Making and Increase Profits

WILEY

Published by John Wiley & Sons, Inc., Hoboken, New Jersey.
Published simultaneously in Canada.

For general information on our other products and services or for technical support, please contact our Customer Care Department within the United States at (800) 762-2974, outside the United States at (317) 572-3993 or fax (317) 572-4002.

Wiley also publishes its books in a variety of electronic formats. Some content that appears in print may not be available in electronic formats. For more information about Wiley products, visit our web site at www.wiley.com.

Library of Congress Cataloging-in-Publication Data is Available:

ISBN 9781119984047 (Hardback)
ISBN 9781119984054 (ePDF)
ISBN 9781119984061 (ePub)

Cover Design: Wiley
Cover Image: © local_doctor/Shutterstock

SKY10044634_031723

I dedicate this book to humanity's curious, enthusiastic, and prosocial nature.

It's time to shine!

CONTENTS

Introduction: How a Flood in Johnstown, Pennsylvania Inspired Computational Leadership

In 1880, Henry Clay Frick, chairperson of the Carnegie Steel Company and one of the wealthiest people in the world, led a group of investors in purchasing an abandoned reservoir, which they converted into the South Fork Fishing and Hunting Club. It was a playground for the wealthy elite of the day. A place where they could escape the chaos of America's industrial revolution.

Unfortunately, during development, leadership made three doomed decisions regarding repairs to the reservoir's dam—which was then the largest earthen dam in the world. They lowered the dam by over three feet to make its top wide enough for a two-lane road, they added debris-gathering fish screens in the spillway to maintain fish stocks, and they decided not to replace drainage pipes, which were sold off for scrap by the previous owner. The Club's leaders took these actions despite continued warnings from engineers that the dam's modifications and insufficient repairs were creating a situation for catastrophic failure.[1]

The stage was set for crisis, and in less than a decade of purchasing the dam, the possibility of failure became a horrific reality on May 31, 1889. After record-breaking rainfall, the dam broke and my hometown—Johnstown, Pennsylvania—was leveled with 20 million tons of water, killing 2,209 people and accounting for approximately $534 million in damage (in 2023 money). The flood, at the time, was the worst disaster in US history. It utterly devastated the city, and it left an ugly scar on Henry Clay Frick's legacy simply because he was too narcissistic, too short-term focused, and too stubborn to change his self-interested behavior.[2]

So what does this have to do with computational leadership? It's a cautionary tale against two perilous gambles: ignoring data and science, and shirking investment in necessary technology. These are the unsustainable choices of impoverished leaders prioritizing business as usual over lasting resilience. They're the decisions of people succumbing to the dark side of leadership.

Fortunately, the future of leadership introduced in this book is much brighter. Innovative leaders will unlock new, sustainable, and equitable ways of creating value with a fantastic array of digital tools and techniques. They will gain next-level vision to make better choices in times of complexity and uncertainty. And they will create environments where self-interest and group interest work in unison.

LEADING WITH DIGITAL VISION

To get started, first ask yourself how you want to be remembered. Do you want to leave an infamous Frick-like legacy, or do you want to break new ground that ushers in remarkable changes to business and society? Because the true standout leaders display vision, courage, curiosity, resourcefulness, sustainability, and a keen sense of experimentation. They clearly articulate key questions related to core business and use all available data, science, and tech—while leveraging their human and social capital—to create previously unseen opportunities. The great ones, in short, work like gifted scientists searching for deeper meaning and truth.

A direct path to this bright future is through what I call computational leadership science (CLS)—that is, the study and application of leadership at the intersection of trailblazing science and technology, well-established research, and invaluable knowledge gleaned from practice. As I mentioned in a March 2022 *Harvard Business Review* article, "CLS allows businesses to better anticipate, address, mitigate, and even benefit from the tidal waves of disruption one's organization is going to experience in the months and years ahead."[3]

You can think of CLS as a set of digital golf clubs, and CLS advisors like me as digital golf pros helping you make the right choices. During the early stages of digital leadership, for example, a wellspring of "digital clubs" emerged. There is now an overabundance of choice, with hundreds of "all hype, no help" clubs set to derail your performance. Leaders, metaphorically speaking, might end up buying an overpriced driver when a less expensive alternative works just as well. Even worse, without a digital golf pro, they may end up using the wrong club for the shot, like someone hacking away with a $2,000 driver at a ball in a sand trap.

CLS and CLS advisors will help you avoid these problems and take your performance to the next level with well-chosen tools. In the chapters to come, you will learn both what clubs are available and which one to use for each shot. And, by the end of the book, it's my goal to make you a CLS-driven leader—or leader in the making—prepared for society's increasingly digital future.

This book, therefore, is not a technology-centered gospel espousing the unquestionable value of "all things tech, all the time." You're the leaders and followers exhibiting agency, and you're at the center of this CLS revolution. The shot is yours to take, not the machine's. As the digital golf pro with thorough knowledge of both the course and the different clubs, I will simply help you choose the right club and make suggestions on how to use it.

THE BEAUTY OF LEADERSHIP

Before diving deeper into CLS and how it can turbocharge your value, let me explain why I'm fascinated by leadership.

> LEADERSHIP IS SCALABLE. Leadership can orchestrate everything from two innovators in a garage poised to disrupt an entire market to worldwide pandemic responses saving millions of lives. The largest employer on the planet—the US Department of Defense—coordinates the efforts of over 2.91 million employees, for example. Leadership, simply put, is present in

the smallest groups, the largest groups, and everything in between.

LEADERSHIP IS FLEXIBLE. From cold wars to warm relations, leadership makes a difference. This adaptive process is able to adjust across a varied organizational landscape. Leadership can be used to battle for market share, to cultivate prosocial HR practices, to explore new entrepreneurial opportunities, and to refine established ways of working. Leadership styles and practices also vary according to the situation. At times, collective and transformation leadership emerges; at other times, directive and transactional leadership comes to the forefront. Like water in a river, leadership boosts coordination by aligning with—and eventually shaping—the situation.

LEADERSHIP IS UNIVERSAL. Leadership is (and was) present in all known cultures and societies. Leadership is also common across most social species, from primates and wolves to cows and ants. Leadership even occurs between species where humans are the followers: for example, there are fishermen in Brazil who follow dolphins. The dolphins herd schools of mullet to the shore where the fishermen are waiting with nets. The dolphins then strike the water with their heads or tails to signal when the fishermen should cast their nets. The outcome of this rudimentary but effective leadership dynamic is a mutual payoff: the fishermen get a large haul of easily caught fish and the dolphins get individual fish separated from the school.[4,5]

This is the beauty and value of leadership. It's scalable, flexible, and universal. At the extremes, leadership can ramp up to vast numbers, connecting people across the globe—or scale down to dyadic relationships where unique interpersonal bonds drive grassroots change. Leadership can also establish cooperation between groups one day and transform to defend against outside enemies the next. Effective leaders can then adjust these factors to meet the needs of, and influence, any situation, from green policy and supply chains to financial practices and crisis management. The key is adopting the right tools and techniques to harness the scalable, flexible, and universal power of leadership.

DEFINING (DIGITAL) LEADERSHIP

The first step in learning how to fully wield the power of leadership is clearly understanding what it is and is not. A leader, of course, is an individual, while leadership is a process incorporating leaders, followers, and the situation. Leadership, as a people process, dives into volatility, uncertainty, complexity, and ambiguity—VUCA environments—to innovate solutions and discover new opportunities. An effective leadership process eats VUCA for breakfast using all available tools, techniques, and human-social capital at its disposal.

Also, leadership is typically thought of as a "soft" intuitive skill, while management is a "hard" science, but those lines are blurring, and the days of purely intuitive decisions are over. Technological innovation, (big) data, an army of analytical experts, and savvy leaders are vaporizing the idea that leadership is purely a soft skill. Gone are the days of winging it based on gut feelings—at least for those who want to remain competitive and sustainable. Instead, business and society is on the cusp of a shift where ALL aspects of leadership—from ensuring inclusive engagement to creating sustainable supply chains—are overhauled through the application of computational methods, including AI, network analysis, predictive modeling, and simulations.

Most leadership processes are starting to incorporate this approach where—at the very least—intuitive decisions are data informed. Netflix, for example, combines advanced viewer analytics with years of experience when selecting content.[6] This evolution of leadership means the use of data, science, and tech is a must-have for leaders wanting to improve profits, increase growth, streamline operations, and generally optimize decision-making.

THE DAWN OF COMPUTATIONAL LEADERSHIP SCIENCE

Though the critical imperative for leaders to use all available data, science, and tech is nothing new—as the opening Frick example proves—society's current spring of innovation is rapidly increasing the effectiveness of leadership. Data and tech are providing leaders with the power to use social capital and drive change like never before. It's truly a fundamental shift in leadership.

Leaders now have the digital clubs to avoid the traps of an analogue past. They can go beyond old-school practices such as "come back to the office because I said so" leadership, and they can break "good enough" habits inhibiting exploration and growth. These are post-digital leaders who have the clubs AND the ability to use them. They combine knowledge gleaned from practice, innovative technology, and decades of leadership research to make and save organizations billions—while driving unprecedented levels of innovation and sustainability.

CLS will help leaders strengthen interpersonal relationships and morale in the era of remote working, and it will increase diversity, equity, and inclusion by separating a leader's biased wants from their actual needs in hiring and promotion. CLS will help mitigate fragile, just-in-time supply chains and corner the market on complexity with the power of quantum computing—the so-called quantum advantage. CLS-driven leaders will also connect and coordinate a global network of collective intelligence to tackle society's biggest challenges.

CLS, simply put, is the new standard for leadership excellence in a time of unprecedented economic, environmental, social, and technological disruption. Hesitate, and the near future is going to feel alien and uncertain. Be proactive with CLS, and you'll guide sustainable change with purposeful intent.

A ROAD MAP FOR BUILDING YOUR CLS CAPACITY

The goal of this book is to ensure you stay on this sustainable path to growth. In Part I, we'll explore key challenges affecting every organization. First, I'll review what we know about CLS in relation to leadership development, employee engagement, DEI (diversity, equity, and inclusion), sustainability, crisis leadership, and employee health and well-being. I'll then discuss how leaders can use CLS to discover hidden opportunities embedded in these core organizational factors. Finally, I end each chapter with interviews of senior leaders from IBM, JPMorgan Chase, Microsoft, WebMD, and more who shared with me how they're using CLS to grow and succeed.

By reading Part I as a series of steps, you'll better understand how all of the different data and tech puzzle pieces fit together to form a holistic view of organizational leadership. That said, if you prefer, feel free to read only the sections specific to your needs. Just keep in mind that in skipping any of the chapters in Part I you might miss out on cross-functional seeds for growing next-level solutions.

In Part II, I'll provide you with a method for both clearly defining any challenge you're facing and assembling CLS teams to co-create opportunities. This is where you unleash the full potential of CLS. You'll expand your set of digital clubs, knowing which one to use for each shot and how to use it. From strengthening personal relationships to improving strategic decision-making, CLS will help you redefine what it means to be a great leader.

My ultimate (optimistic) goal with this book is ensuring that no one ever again relies on the dated and dangerous practices of people like Henry Clay Frick. Instead, I want you to carve out a new and innovative leadership niche that's connected, sustainable, and obsessed with stakeholder value. At the end of the day, CLS-driven leaders have an opportunity to make a distinct impact on the timeline of leadership, and you can be part of this renaissance. Now, let's begin your journey.

PART I

LEARNING ABOUT COMPUTATIONAL LEADERSHIP

CHAPTER 1

Developing the Roberto Clementes of Leadership

One of my joys is diving into the backstories of leaders. I look for trends in their progress the same way I study baseball to see what separates the great from the good. I want to know what next-level leaders do to elevate above the average. Figuratively speaking, I want to know what makes them the Roberto Clementes of leadership—a baseball great known for his tireless contributions both on and off the field.

I find that the Clementes of leadership know how to deliver results in the face of extreme adversity. They have a keen sense of their core values, they work hard AND smart, they make sacrifices, they prioritize stakeholder value, and they continuously take on board new information to improve their game. They also know that leadership development (LD) is a focal point for greatness.

Whether it's onboarding high potentials, growing a network of informal leaders, or grooming the next generation of senior leaders, LD drives an organization's trajectory. It makes a significant impact on leadership capacity, and leadership capacity makes a significant impact on performance. LD, simply put, is at the center of sustainable growth.

The goal of this chapter is to help you nurture this growth with the latest in science and tech. We'll start with summarizing existing work to give you an idea of what experts know about LD. We'll then get to the details of how you can use computational leadership science (CLS) to foster next-level leadership. Finally, in the Q&A section, we'll see how IBM—one of the best at developing talent—is taking steps to boost its LD with digital innovations.

What We Know about Leadership Development

The concept and practice of LD has been around for decades, and experts have amassed a great deal of information in that time. I want to briefly touch on this mountain of information because it's a raw material waiting to be refined into 21st-century knowledge.

Interestingly, the current state of LD is similar to the premise of Michael Lewis's 2003 book *Moneyball: The Art of Winning an Unfair Game*, where the Oakland Athletics baseball team paired an endless flow of baseball stats with advanced analytics to build a highly competitive team on a small budget. Its 2002 payroll was only $44 million, and yet it was able to find hidden talent and compete with teams like the Yankees, which spent over $125 million on the "best" players that year. The Oakland A's did more with less and changed the way Major League Baseball does business by stepping away from traditional baseball wisdom. They "Moneyballed" the game. And now you can do same—you can Moneyball LD—by tapping into the endless stream of data flowing through your organization. It'll revolutionize how you develop the Roberto Clementes of leadership.[1]

To start this digital revolution, let's first explore what research and practice already knows.

> We know that aligning needs with LD offerings makes organizations robust and sustainable. Getting LD right is the foundation for healthy growth while getting it wrong creates a downward spiral of bad leaders creating bad leadership processes selecting for worse leaders and worse leadership processes. It's similar to making copies of copies and losing resolution over time. This is why practitioners and researchers in the know place so much importance on LD, and why it's a fast-growing market with an estimated value over $350 billion. As organizations have become aware of how critical LD is to their success, they have loosened their purse strings, and providers have rushed in to help. This dynamic sets the stage for a market filled with innovative products and services for taking your LD skills to the next level (provided you choose the right tools).[2]

WE KNOW THERE'S A DIFFERENCE BETWEEN DEVELOPING LEADERS AND DEVELOPING LEADERSHIP. One aspect of LD to consider when shopping around for products and services relates to the difference between a leader as a person and leadership as a process. Whereas LEADER development focuses on boosting individual-level traits such as empathy and confidence, LEADERSHIP development focuses on developing group-level competencies for overcoming challenges and capitalizing on opportunity. For example, your group might need tools for developing shared leadership processes to empower employees and boost cross-functional performance.[3]

WE KNOW LD NEEDS TO BE HABITUAL. Another defining aspect of LD is the importance of investing in continual improvement. Consider the difference between going to the gym once a week versus making it a habit. Go once a week, and you might get sore, but you won't get stronger. But if you regularly work out, and you pursue new exercises and learn how to focus on different muscle groups, you'll get stronger and more agile. The same is true for LD; you have to make LD habitual if you want to increase your effectiveness.

WE KNOW LD TOOLS NEED TO BE JUDGED ON THEIR ABILITY TO INFLUENCE SPECIFIC OUTCOMES. Effective tools should work to drive the organization's strategy. For example, they should develop a strong pipeline for high potentials to rise and add continued value, and they should work to enhance critical factors such as diversity, equity, and inclusion (DEI). LD applications should also focus on real, practical challenges, develop the whole person not just specific competencies, and uncover a deeper, service-oriented meaning to leadership.[4]

WE KNOW LD IS A SYSTEMIC PRIORITY. The data shows that most people are worried about leadership's ability to adapt and perform under pressure, especially during these uncertain times. Here are some compelling insights regarding the scope of concern:

- LEADERS ARE CONCERNED. Korn Ferry conducted a survey of almost 7,500 senior leaders and found that only 17% were confident they had the necessary capabilities to achieve their organizations' strategic priorities.

- EMPLOYEES ARE CONCERNED. A global survey of 4,000 employees conducted by Gartner found that only 50% were confident in their leaders' ability to create an inspiring vision of the future.

- EXTERNAL STAKEHOLDERS ARE CONCERNED. Findings from the 2022 Edelman Trust Barometer—a survey of over 36,000 respondents across 28 countries—found that CEOs are expected to develop skills to "shape conversation and policy on jobs and the economy (76%), wage inequity (73%), technology and automation (74%) and global warming and climate change (68%)."

Leadership, in other words, is mandated to deliver on all aspects of business and society, but most stakeholders—including leaders—are worried that LD hasn't kept pace with situational demands.[5,6,7]

WE KNOW THERE'S A LARGE GAP BETWEEN WHAT LEADERS SHOULD DEVELOP AND WHAT'S TYPICALLY ON OFFER IN THE LD MARKET. Experiential learning, for example, is a core theme in LD. Practitioners have advanced guided methods of learning through experience for decades. Yes, of course, a structured experiential approach is an important aspect of LD. Having opportunities to engage in concrete experiences and then learning how to reflect and apply this experience across a broader range of scenarios strengthens autonomy, confidence, and ultimately effectiveness. However, emerging research suggests that experiential learning can also lead to overconfidence stemming from excessive attention and praise, unnecessary conflict between those chosen for such LD initiatives and those left out of the loop, and emotional exhaustion—a "too much of a good thing" effect—where participants are simply overtrained. In practice, though this experiential concept feels right, research is telling a much more nuanced story where practical training for a select few can lead to toxic outcomes overall. Certain leaders may feel more confident, but the overall leadership system is not well prepared for challenges and opportunities.[8]

What We Don't Know about Leadership Development

This LD gap is problematic because it leads to blind spots in our understanding. Cultivating talent over time, for instance, is often imprecise and prone to failure. The following are four of these blind spots holding up much-needed improvements to LD.[9]

> The scholar-practitioner blind spot: Whereas the practice side of LD traditionally relies on intuitive, well-packaged ideas, scientists traditionally rely on simplified analytical models that allow for a deep but not always practical understanding of LD. Leadership scholars know that experiential learning has its limitations, for example, but they don't typically have the practical experience to devise better alternatives. This divide between scholars and practitioners makes it difficult to create useful *and* scientifically valid tools.[10]

> The temporal blind spot: Leaders are working with LD products and services lacking sufficient power to improve leaders and leadership over time. This temporal neglect is like going to a gym without a plan of action. You're not sure what to work on, how to work on it, or when to work on it. The results—like at the gym—are bad habits such as engaging in useless exercises, not keeping a schedule, and the potential for long-term injury.

> You'll likely struggle to effectively develop talent and face huge losses when these bad habits emerge. For example, grooming the next generation of leaders without understanding the long-term impact of your choices can select for toxic leader traits. People tend to gravitate toward charismatic leaders given their ability to communicate a vision and inspire—especially during crises. There are countless self-help books helping budding leaders channel their inner Steve Jobs for this very reason. However, this trait also has a dark side, which leads to costly self-promotion at the expense of teams, divisions, and even the entire organization.[11]

THE MULTILEVEL BLIND SPOT: LD experts don't have a firm grasp on understanding how leaders systematically influence behavior and performance at the team level, the department level, and so on. Without this multilevel perspective, it's impossible to predict whether leaders are going build resilient teams and develop high potentials as a result of LD programs.[12]

THE DEI BLIND SPOT: LD experts also lack a deep understanding of demographically inclusive development. Just because traditional LD programs (potentially) worked for white male leaders that doesn't mean the same programs will work for the broad spectrum of modern leaders. Developing individualistic leader traits in a collectivist culture, for example, can easily backfire.[13]

Getting rid of the blind spots and reliably improving LD outcomes requires all the data and expertise you can get your hands on. I guarantee performance directors developing the next baseball greats aren't doing it intuitively. They're sending their athletes to biomechanics labs, using data to develop customized workout regimes and diets, and working with sports psychologists to overcome adversity. An athlete on a $100 million contract isn't developed using mental notes and jotting down ideas on paper; their development is based on the latest in science and technology.[14]

And just as fans want more from players, stakeholders want more and more from leaders. This is why developing talent with CLS is a must for continued success. An ability to combine state-of-the-art tech, unprecedented amounts of data, and proven leadership science will turbocharge performance. You'll develop the new Clementes of leadership, and you'll do this by Moneyballing LD.

CLS-RELEVANT TECHNOLOGY

Similar to the holistic, data-informed precision of Moneyball baseball, you need to know how LD initiatives work over time and how they influence performance across various levels and segments of your organization. You also need to know how LD initiatives can incorporate a demographically diverse understanding of the world. It's a fast-paced, high-stakes environment filled with opportunities for CLS-driven leaders who can use an unprecedented convergence of data, experience, science, and tech.

If you are ready to take this step, then here are three challenges you need to address:

What Data to Collect and Why

Attaining high-quality data is a crucial first step for fundamentally improving LD because it allows you to systematically create powerful, purposeful, and lasting initiatives. Without high-quality data all the sophisticated analytics and technology in the world mean very little. In fact, using cutting-edge analytics and tech with low-quality data can lead to catastrophic decisions. An organization driven by fads and hype—rather than science and high-quality data—could end up homogenizing LD when diversity is necessary. For example, scientists analyzing leader performance might find a link between charisma and effectiveness—during a pandemic, for example—which practitioners then package and promote as THE LD factor for success. Unfortunately, decision-makers going all in on charisma will likely come to find their organization is overrun with self-promoting, overconfident, and generally toxic individuals.[15,16]

This data-impoverished approach not accounting for the complexity of LD makes it impossible to set up reliable initiatives. Instead, you're likely reinventing a very expensive wheel every couple of years as fads fail and go out of fashion. This is why high-quality data is crucial for developing the Clementes of leadership.

At the very least, given the organizational blind spots mentioned earlier, you need to collect temporal, multilevel, and demographically diverse LD data using a combination of subjective and objective measures. For example, Guardian Life Insurance Company, a Fortune 500 company with LD programs consistently ranked among the best, collects OBJECTIVE temporal LD data on leader retention and advancement as well as SUBJECTIVE temporal data on their self-reported knowledge gained from LD initiatives and the growth of their personal networks.[17]

To address the multilevel blind spot, Virgin Media O2 emphasizes a team-oriented understanding of LD. This includes collecting SUBJECTIVE multilevel data of LD such as employee engagement, employee net promoter score (eNPS), and employee pride. In the same vein, Associa, the largest community management company in the US with 11,000 employees spread across the country, tracks OBJECTIVE multilevel outcomes such as employee promotion rate. The logic is that developing great leaders increase employee retention and encourage others to strive for advancement in the organization.[18,19]

Regarding DEI, companies such as Amazon and Maersk are using data-driven technologies such as gamification to improve diversity in their LD pipelines. Amazon, as part of its "Catapult" initiation, is developing high-potential female leaders using a simulated business environment to practice newly acquired leadership skills in a safe but lifelike environment. The goal is seeing more female leaders spread throughout the organization. Similarly, Maersk developed an online game in partnership with a gaming studio to help managers improve their hiring practices and avoid cognitive biases. The game follows users through the hiring process, alerting them when bias might emerge. Pitfalls such as writing gendered job adverts are highlighted by the game, and leaders are prompted to stop, think, and avoid. Both Maersk and Amazon can then use the underlying data streaming in from their respective initiatives to identify real-time LD needs and encourage development in low-risk—sometimes simulated—environments.[20,21]

Ultimately, paradigm-shifting excellence in LD requires you to cover all of the bases—temporal, multilevel, DEI, objective, and subjective. Collecting diverse sources of high-quality data is essential if you want to go beyond the horizon of anecdotes and intuition (see Table 1.1 for examples).

With this varied approach to data collection, you grind a superior lens for seeing hidden insights. You might find that even though leaders subjectively see value in your LD activities, little benefit is objectively extending out to diverse individuals and teams in the form of

Table 1.1 Data examples for holistic, CLS-driven leadership development.

LD Data Examples	Temporal Examples	Multilevel Examples	Diversity Examples
Objective Examples	Leader retention rate	Employee promotion rate	Leader ability to recognize and avoid gendered language
Subjective Examples	Leader self-reported growth of personal networks	Employee net promotor score (eNPS)	Leader self-reported grasp of DEI values and benefits

promotions and other growth opportunities. Recognizing such short-comings with high-quality data helps you improve return on investment (ROI) and clarifies your path to sustainable growth.

What Tech to Pair with the LD Data

The future of CLS-driven LD is indeed a continual process of collecting diverse data, which is combined with innovative technology to create initiatives tailored to the real-time needs of leaders, teams, departments, and the organization as a whole.

Table 1.1 serves as a framework for clarifying which tech to use and why. Each box is a data blind spot that both leadership scholars and practitioners on the ground recognize. You can use this framework to systematically leverage tech on your way to Moneyballing LD. Here's an example of how you can collect and use this data:

> Empathy—the ability to understand and share how someone else feels—is one of the most important leadership skills to develop. This is especially true now that work environments are becoming more asynchronous, remote, and thankfully diverse. Organizations with empathic leaders are more engaged, innovative, and inclusive. Higher levels of empathy among leaders also increase employee retention and financial ROI. Given the importance of

empathy, it behooves leaders and LD specialists to use every bit of data, science, and tech available to nurture and spread this trait throughout their organization.[22,23,24,25]

This is why companies such as Hilton are using advancements in tech such as VR to re-create the customer experience and to meet their ever-expanding training and development needs. As Jennifer Rinck, Vice President of Learning put it, "Once you experience [VR] . . . and how much it can build empathy and change behavior, it's really the best tool by which we can simulate a real experience." Leaders don't have to read dry articles on empathy or go through less-than-engaging exercises on a computer. Instead, they can jump into an on-demand virtual world to practice realistic scenarios. It's a low-risk, safe, and immersive environment to develop the Clementes of leadership.[26]

For example, you can combine "VR facial emotion recognition" training (an objective measure of empathic ability where participants attempt to identify facial emotions in highly immersive virtual environments) with subjective self-report measures of empathy such as the "Interpersonal Reactivity Index" to explore subtle differences in perceived versus actual ability. You'll likely find that certain leaders will rate themselves high on empathy yet score low on the objective VR measure. This is perhaps a sign of overconfidence—a known problem among leaders—where needing to always project competence muddies the waters of self-awareness. On the other hand, some leaders will score low on self-reported empathy and high on the objective measure, pointing to an underestimation of ability.[27,28,29]

Though both obviously require attention, the starting points are quite different. LD professionals can use this VR system to surface these different patterns and introduce training programs to either decrease hubris or increase self-confidence. For example, you can have overconfident leaders do a "pre-mortem"—prior to an immersive emotion recognition task, leaders are asked to assume they'll perform poorly and explain this outcome. Research shows this technique to think about possible mistakes in their logic reduces overconfidence and improves decision-making. And leaders underestimating their empathic ability can boost their self-awareness with proven exercises such as explicitly giving themselves credit for performance outcomes and constructive self-talk to combat their inner critic. Now, with VR, leaders can work on these opportunities for improvement anytime, anywhere in a realistic environment.[30,31]

Going further, emerging technology allows leaders to literally "swap bodies" with virtual colleagues. They can practice skills such as active listening and perspective-taking and then swap bodies with their virtual colleague and watch their performance from the other person's perspective. The technology also supplies semantic analytics and personalized tips for improvement. It's a 3D environment to see and hear how others perceive you, and it's the closest thing we have to a functional Holodeck (for the Trekkies out there).[32]

Finally, note this is just a small taste of the tech you can leverage to boost LD. There's obviously more to developing leaders and leadership. We'll explore this expansive LD landscape and how you can wrap digital tools around any development goal in Chapter 8.

Unlocking Insights from Existing, Sometimes Hidden, Data

The final challenge for Moneyballing LD and developing the Clementes of leadership is harnessing the neglected reservoirs of data in your organization. Forrester, a research and advisory company, for example, estimates that up to 70% of all data goes unused in enterprises. Businesses either don't have the necessary technology to access this resource or they lack the necessary expertise to refine the data into actionable insights.[33]

Fortunately, you can unlock this untapped potential by building diverse teams. Data engineers, for instance, are helpful when it comes to setting up ways to securely collect, store, and manage data. As Google puts it, "a data engineer should be able to design, build, operationalize, secure, and monitor data-processing systems with a particular emphasis on security and compliance; scalability and efficiency; reliability and fidelity; and flexibility and portability." They are broadly responsible for the infrastructure and architecture supporting higher-level LD analytics and applications. In short, you likely have vast amounts of LD data hidden throughout your organization, and data engineers will help you find this valuable resource.[34]

Data scientists are another must-have member for your CLS team. They are highly skilled in building analytical and predictive models using the data received from the engineers. Their duties, according to Oracle, "include developing strategies for analyzing data, preparing data for analysis, exploring, analyzing, and visualizing data, building models with data using programming languages, such as Python and R, and deploying models into applications." Compared to engineers, they focus more on introducing state-of-the-art methods for using data resources. For example, they can help you find new ways of capturing and analyzing data related to empathy training and its impact on factors such as employee retention and productivity.[35]

Finally, data analysts—in this case, social and leadership scientists with analytical backgrounds—are essential for helping you define the challenge or opportunity and making sense out of the data. They're the tip of the spear when it comes to developing actionable insights from (hidden) data. Their role is finding and applying relevant patterns in existing data as well as working with engineers and data scientists on plans for finding and analyzing new types of data to deliver a continuous stream of actionable insights. For example, IBM deployed a team of analysts—working in tandem with engineers and data scientists—to create a digitized platform for specialized training and micro-learning tailored to leaders' existing skills, behavior, and personality. By connecting these computational dots, IBM is taking LD to the next level.[36]

As a final note before moving onto my Q&A with IBM, remember that you don't have to be an engineer, data scientist, analyst, and decision-makers all rolled up in one person. That's impossible! Instead, you are the CLS leader orchestrating change. You find the pains and opportunities, the blind spots, and the diverse talent to reach new heights. CLS is your opportunity to create a shared leadership environment with the power to fundamentally shift the future of LD.

With that in mind, let's check out how IBM is coordinating its LD initiatives.

LEADERSHIP DEVELOPMENT Q&A WITH IBM

"Our priority . . . is to embed IBM's Growth Behaviors across our entire portfolio—helping leaders at every level understand how to develop and improve these behaviors."
—Sofia Lamuraglia, Director of Leadership Development, IBM

It was my pleasure to interview Sofia Lamuraglia, Director of IBM Leadership Development, and Jennifer Sevilla Montana, IBM Executive Development Consultant.

The IBM Corporation is a large US-based multinational technology corporation with over 250,000 employees worldwide. To train and develop such a large and diverse workforce, IBM relies heavily on LD. As stated on its website, "IBM's leaders are central to our transformation journey. As we develop leaders from aspiring managers to senior executives, we strive to create innovative, experiential, and practical learning opportunities and resources that foster an understanding of their role and purpose, while preparing them for an environment that is increasingly collaborative, self-directed, and agile." This central focus on LD and the corporation's digital DNA makes IBM a perfect candidate for exploring CLS-driven approaches to developing leaders from junior employees to senior executives.

Q: What LD challenge or opportunity is a priority for your organization?

A: Our CEO has defined a clear strategy focused on hybrid cloud and AI and our commitment to driving accelerated business growth. We know that in order to execute on this business strategy, we need to transform our culture, and leadership behaviors are a key element of bringing that culture to life. As a result of our recent transformation, we have articulated a culture formula that drives IBM's culture: purpose + values + behaviors. It's why we exist (purpose), what we believe (values), and how we act (behaviors). IBM's Growth Behaviors is the HOW we bring our purpose and values to life. Our priority for the LD organization is to embed IBM's

Growth Behaviors across our entire portfolio—helping leaders at every level understand how to develop and improve these behaviors.

Q: What specific question(s) do you have regarding your organization's ability to address LD?

A: The first important question is: How do we drive behavior change at scale, quickly, acknowledging the many competing priorities that are consuming the time and attention of our users? The other questions are about moving from compliance to commitment: How can we use data to show IBM leaders the value of attending our LD offerings? How do we help IBMers see the value of investing their time in the culture transformation necessary to drive business growth? Relatedly, how do we show the connection between LD initiatives and our transformational outcomes? Finally, how do we help leaders use LD data to change their mindset and behaviors as well as their teams' to align with IBM's broad cultural transformation?

Q: What specific expectations do you have about what's influencing your organization's ability to address LD?

A: The biggest influences on our ability to address LD opportunities at IBM come down to the pace at which we are growing combined with COVID-19. For instance, we have a large number of new IBMers and leaders who have never been to an IBM office. Even though we've focused on [leadership development] behaviors from the start, they are new for many IBMers. Also, the need to manically focus on our clients and growth and execute with speed can sometimes get in the way of the *how*. Under pressure, people sometimes revert to what they know and what has worked in the past for them, which can get in the way of displaying new behaviors.

Q: What data and tech are you using to inform LD strategies and resources?

A: We use data and technology in various ways to help inform our LD strategy, resources, and approaches. At the organizational level, we use enterprise collaboration tools like Slack with Watson AI analytics to keep an open dialog between leaders and employees. Always-on channels such as "Ask-Me-Anything" allow us to keep a real-time pulse on the needs that leaders should adapt to meet.

We also rely on our "Annual Engagement Survey" and pulse survey data to inform us of the areas of culture and leadership that need immediate attention. We conduct yearly business impact analysis with the Annual Engagement Survey results to measure the impact of our leadership development offerings. In 2021, we found that leaders who have obtained or are eligible for the LD badge called "License to Lead" score 1.6 points higher in the Engagement Index, 4.8 points higher in the Inclusion Index, and were better evaluated by their teams in the leadership-related engagement survey questions.

To accelerate our culture transformation effort, the "IBM Growth Behaviors" were embedded into what we look for when we hire, how we recognize and reward IBMers, how we measure engagement and performance, and how we assess, select, and develop leaders. To that end, we aligned leadership assessments to the behaviors and use that data to inform personal and organizational learning plans, as well as LD strategic priorities. For instance, 360° feedback scores were used to send learning nudges by Slack to leaders based on their growth areas. Leaders who scored high on the behaviors were selected to share stories or lead breakout sessions discussing their behaviors. Finally, the overall 360° feedback scores informed the content of deep-dive sessions for our senior leaders.

At the leader/manager level, we also track metrics to gauge the impact of the leadership development portfolio. The most recent measure shows that managers who have completed at least one LD learning in the past two years are 20% LESS likely to be off track in our "Leadership Indicator" factors.

We also reply on participant feedback from program surveys to inform continuous content improvements across the LD portfolio. We use data-driven techniques to support a pull versus push content strategy for the Leadership Academy, a one-stop-shop platform for all leadership resources. A search dashboard allows our team to monitor what leaders want and adjust our homepage content accordingly. The dashboard also allows us to proactively highlight content aligned to key HR events during the year.

Q: What drove your data and tech choices (e.g., personal decision, team decision, data scientist decision, using what's available, some sort of systematic process for selecting data and tech)?

A: Our culture transformation effort played a role in the type of data available to us. Embedding the IBM Growth Behaviors into what we look for when we hire, how we recognize and reward IBMers, how we measure engagement and performance, and how we assess, select, and develop leaders provides us with new data sets and therefore new opportunities to engage and develop our leaders.

We also work with IBM data scientists to help us to understand what data is available and how we can utilize that data to support our goals—for example, demonstrating an LD offerings impact or how best to drive targeted interventions.

Q: What sort of data and/or tech are you using to track LD initiatives over time?

A: We do a yearly business impact study with the Annual Engagement Survey, and starting next year we'll have the opportunity to see year-over-year improvement in the leadership assessment data to gauge the impact of our leadership development interventions and enablement efforts. As mentioned earlier, managers who have completed at least one LD learning in the past two years are 20% less likely to be off track in our Leadership Indicator. Likewise, our data, which we share with IBMers, indicates that leaders attending LD training show significant improvements in critical factors such as providing ongoing feedback to employees, ensuring feedback leads to change, showing more care as a person, and removing obstacles.

Q. What sort of data and/or tech are you using to track LD at multiple levels?

A: We use all the available data and tech mentioned earlier (engagement and pulse surveys, sentiment analysis, 360° feedback data, impact analysis) as well as aggregated insights from coaching partners and people analytics like attrition and career progression.

Q: What sort of data and/or tech are you using to track DEI aspects of your initiatives?

A: Our DEI programs are tracked and measured at multiples levels the same way, using the same data mentioned earlier. As mentioned, leaders who have obtained or are eligible for the LD badge called "License to Lead" (which includes DEI programs) score 1.6 points higher in the Engagement Index and 4.8 points higher in the Inclusion Index and were better evaluated by their teams in the inclusion questions. We find significant improvements in questions such as "My manager cares about me as a person," "I feel comfortable being myself," "IBM's culture is inclusive," and "I'm treated with respect."

Q: What is the (expected) outcome of your tech-enabled plans for LD?

A: By using data to prioritize areas of focus for our LD offerings and interventions, we are expecting to see accelerated progress on our IBM Growth Behaviors as measured in our engagement survey, pulse survey, and 360° assessments. We are also looking to further personalize and target our LD interventions to ensure leaders are investing time and effort where it's most critical based on IBMers' feedback. Using the data also allows us to drive operational efficiencies from a delivery perspective by scheduling and marketing classes that address our leaders needs and interests. We also expect to see some reduction in attrition for the teams of those leaders displaying these behaviors. Ultimately, the big picture is summed up by Chris Foltz, our VP of Talent Strategy and Experience, "IBM's growth is enabled by our cultural transformation, and we believe that happens through leadership—making LD a critical aspect of our long-term, sustainable success."

Concluding Thoughts about My Interview with Sofia Lamuraglia and Jennifer Sevilla Montana

IBM's approach to LD suggests that it's committed to working "smart and hard" with data and tech. Specifically, working closely with data scientists, the LD group keeps a clear focus on its goals and wraps around the simplest configuration of data and tech—the least amount necessary to generate the greatest impact—in order to gain insights and drive cultural change for growth. IBM is simply too large and the amount of data is too great to explore all possible data and tech avenues. So it instead uses a highly effective "keep it simple" approach based on expert advice to sustain industry-leading employee retention and LD.

I also find IBM's use of "passive data" compelling—for example, analyzing what electronic LD materials people are searching for rather than relying solely on self-report survey data. We know from psychological science that what people say they want and how they actually behave don't always match. Their passive data accounts for that discrepancy.

Collectively, IBM's LD team takes a simple yet data-diverse approach. If leaders want to achieve this next-level CLS intelligence, then they need to find their data-and-tech sweet spot. Doing so provides decision-makers with a mature and focused vision of the future.

CHAPTER 2

Releasing the DEI Talent River

Growing up, I lived in a 10-block immigrant neighborhood where distinct ethnic groups worked together to overcome extreme poverty and the terrible working conditions in the steel mills and coal mines. These courageous individuals created a shared sense of identity and community that left an indelible mark on my life regarding the value of diversity. From experience, I fundamentally know diversity, equity, and inclusion (DEI) is critical to performance in a globalized and uncertain world. It's an opportunity to make simultaneously ethical and financial right choices. As McKinsey recently reported, DEI is "a powerful enabler of business [and social] performance . . . and the likelihood of diverse companies outperforming industry peers on profitability has increased significantly."[1]

DEI is a key factor for organizations looking to improve multiple aspects of their operations, including hiring, retention, and customer satisfaction. It also affects performance in complex and often unseen ways. For example, let's say that you think subconscious biases within your organization are creating hidden patterns of exclusion, such as leaders recruiting people with social backgrounds similar to their own. But how could you know for sure if there's no data to surface the underlying implicit behavior? And even if you do intuitively tap into exclusion, it's extremely difficult to address such challenges in the workplace without understanding how to pull the levers of change.

Computational leadership science (CLS) removes this guesswork so you can consistently improve outcomes. For example, data dashboards can visualize the exclusion of talent to raise awareness. Social science can explain the mechanics of human biases to enrich training programs. And tech can mitigate the problem with tools such as customizable search engines for finding diverse talent hidden in social networks.

This is what CLS is all about in the context of DEI. It's a multi-pronged approach to removing bias. It combines data, science, and tech to fully engage a diverse workforce for next-level growth.

To help you attain this CLS advantage, we'll first explore what we know (and don't know) about DEI. We'll then look at how emerging tools can enhance your effectiveness. Finally, we'll peer under the hood of JPMorgan Chase. Its EMEA (Europe, Middle East, and Africa) Head of DEI shared several compelling insights with me on what the company is doing to lead the way in DEI.

WHO CARES ABOUT DEI

Before we start our exploration, it's important to first understand the scope of concern for DEI.

LEADERS CARE ABOUT DEI. A 2022 Fortune/Deloitte survey found that DEI is the number one concern for CEOs when it comes to stakeholder trust, with 92% of them incorporating DEI into their organization's strategic goals and priorities.[2,3]

EMPLOYEES CARE ABOUT DEI. McKinsey, for instance, used natural language processing to analyze the (positive, negative, and neutral) sentiment of employee reviews on Glassdoor and Indeed. This large data set—representing 15 countries and more than 1,000 companies—indicates that, though many employees see organizations recognizing the value of DEI, those efforts are often *not* seen as leading to more engagement with a diverse workforce.[4]

While employee sentiment regarding diversity in their workplace was 52% positive and 31% negative, employee sentiment regarding inclusivity at work was notably worse, at only 29% positive and 61% negative. In other words, even though organizations are working on diversity, they still have a long way to go. They have to do more than hiring a diverse workforce to fully benefit from DEI. It requires meaningful cooperation and equitable outcomes.

CONSUMERS CARE ABOUT DEI. Regarding racial injustice, a 2020 Edelman's Trust Barometer report found that 64% of US consumers want organizations to get their own house in order and set an example internally. Edelman also found that 60% of US consumers will either buy or boycott a brand depending on how it stands on social (in)justice, and that they expect "brands and companies that issue a statement in support of racial equality to follow it up with concrete action."[5]

SOCIETY CARES ABOUT DEI. A 2022 Eurobarometer survey—the official polling instrument used by the European Union—highlights the region's continued and growing demands for broad, inclusive cooperation. Jutta Urpilainen, the Commissioner for International Partnerships, noted that "the EU's new strategy for sustainable infrastructure investments, the Global Gateway, will further strengthen our international partnerships and contribute to reducing inequalities and achieving the [DEI-oriented] sustainable development goals."[6,7]

A similar trend toward DEI voting and policymaking is emerging in the US. Pew Research finds that diversity is an emerging priority among voters: younger adults are turning out to vote in increasing numbers, and they're particularly interested in issues directly related to DEI. These young, informed, and motivated voters are making a difference in elections outcomes, and that momentum shows no signs of slowing down.[8]

Though there are many debates to be had on this topic, it's clear that organizations ignore DEI at their peril. Yes, there are many hurdles to overcome, but this is an exciting time for using data, science, and tech to engage people at scale. Collectively, from small businesses to intergovernmental organizations, modern leaders have opportunities to leverage the power of DEI to make lasting change in business and society. This level of DEI calls for using all the CLS-driven tools at your disposal—from vast lakes of data to invaluable knowledge gleaned from practice. It's about taking what we know and combining it with advancements in science and technology to remove barriers.

WHAT WE KNOW ABOUT DEI LEADERSHIP

Regarding what we know, let's look at how diversity, equity, and inclusion are defined and how they manifest in organizations.

Diversity "refers to any compositional differences among people within a work unit."[9] This broad definition encompasses a range of human differences, some from birth (e.g., race) some through experience (e.g., education), some more observable (e.g., age), and others less observable (e.g., religion). Leaders at this stage are focused on hiring a diverse workforce—even if that means simply filling low-paying roles with individuals to tick the DEI box.

Equity involves the fairness of policy and practice and "the absences of systemic disparities . . . between groups with different levels of underlying social advantage/disadvantage—that is, wealth, power, or prestige."[10] Here, leaders are leveling up and taking action to remove bias, harassment, and discrimination. DEI now starts to permeate throughout the organization beyond box-tick hiring.

Inclusion is "the degree to which individuals feel a part of critical organizational processes such as access to information and resources, involvement in work groups, and an ability to influence the decision-making process."[11] At this stage, the organization is starting to unleash the full power of DEI. Diverse individuals are hired with a focus on training, development, and leadership succession so the organization goes from talking DEI to living DEI. It becomes part of the organization's core cultural DNA.

Unfortunately, weaving DEI into an organization's culture is not an easy task. According to a *Harvard Business Review* Analytics Services survey of over 1,000 leaders from North America, only "67% of respondents say their organization is, at best, only somewhat successful at creating a workplace that is diverse, equitable, and inclusive," and much of this problem (50%) is attributed to "a lack of leadership commitment."[12]

Here are some facts to help overcome this challenge and encourage commitment:

- WE KNOW HUMAN BIASES HINDER DEI. Biases favoring individuals from historically advantaged groups negatively affect the self-esteem and well-being of disadvantaged individuals. In addition, biases such as the affinity bias—for example, leaders favoring followers like themselves based on factors such as sex, education, and socioeconomic background—locks in unequitable and non-inclusive practices. Similarly, there are biases such as the tendency to hire extroverted individuals even though research has shown that introverts can add as much (if not more) value, or a preference for healthy-looking leaders without any evidence suggesting they'll perform better than less healthy-looking leaders.[13,14,15,16]

- WE KNOW THAT DEI SUFFERS FROM TEMPORAL AND MULTI-LEVEL BLIND SPOTS. Scholars and practitioners alike are unsure how DEI initiatives play out over time or how DEI training actually affects engagement, motivation, satisfaction, and performance at multiple levels of an organization. Experts have some educated guesses, but until recently they lacked the data and tech necessary to move from guesswork to concrete evidence.[17]

- WE KNOW THAT DEI IS A MUST FOR ATTRACTING TALENT. Both minority and non-minority job seekers respond favorably to messages about diversity and descriptions of company DEI philosophy. One survey in the US found that 70% of people searching for a job value a potential employer's commitment to DEI. Another US-based study of more than 250,000 job seekers found that they were "willing to forgo more than $1,000 in wages to work at a place with a more diverse employee base."[18,19]

- WE KNOW THAT DEI BOOSTS PERFORMANCE. For example, research from Deloitte finds that improvements in DEI can produce a nearly 30% increase in the ability to spot and reduce risks, such as risks associated with climate change. And a World

Economic Forum report finds that effective DEI can contribute up to 20% higher rates of innovative output, such as developing greener products and services to meet changing consumer demands. And, as for the bottom line, the same World Economic Forum report finds that diverse groups are better at enhancing market share, and they're 25% to 36% more likely to outperform on profitability.[20,21]

The takeaway from this brief overview of known facts is that DEI creates a competitive advantage. The evidence is undeniable. Unfortunately, practitioners and researchers are unsure how to implement, leverage, and sustain this valuable resource. Following are some blind spots in our knowledge.

WHAT WE DON'T KNOW ABOUT DEI LEADERSHIP

Put bluntly, most white males experience minimal barriers in the workplace, whereas many individuals who are not white males often experience systemic, though extremely subtle, barriers—from not being promoted to not being included in informal social activities with colleagues. These outcomes result from the fact that, since hiring decisions have such a large impact on the success of an organization, it's all too easy for recruiters and hiring managers to consider it the safest bet to select candidates they feel they can relate to or candidates who would be a good fit with the established workforce.

Since these choices often derive from unconscious biases, the cause and effect is hidden and thus extremely difficult to root out. One approach toward ameliorating this pervading factor is to train leaders to avoid the pitfalls of bias, discrimination, and exclusion. Unfortunately, we know little about the efficacy of these interventions, from both research and practice perspectives.[22]

For example, we don't yet have definitive answers to the following questions:

- Does DEI training actually decrease discrimination and stigmatization in the workforce?

- Does DEI training increase a sense of belonging over time and at every level of the organization?

- If DEI training is effective, then how is it effective? How can leaders systematically replicate positive outcomes?

Leaders also lack a robust set of metrics to measure and understand DEI outcomes related to organizational performance, such as the effect on services ratings, reputation ratings, and governance ratings. As such, DEI initiatives are often seen as a cost rather than a benefit. The sheer truth is you need data and tech if you want to unleash the full power of DEI!

CLS-Driven DEI Leadership

To help you achieve next-level DEI leadership, we're going to explore three important challenges in the employee's journey: getting noticed and entering the organization, becoming a respected member of the team, and having an equal say in decision-making. We'll explore solutions for removing barriers to progress at every step and how you can use these insights to drive change.

Challenge: Recruiting and Hiring

Diverse talent pools help you find the right people to manage complex and ever-changing challenges. In fact, rather than calling it a talent pool, which sounds static, I suggest you think of it as a talent river constantly flowing into your organization. Like rivers, everyone has a unique source, such as gender, race, and ethnicity. We also have tributaries adding to our diversity over time, such as education, marital status, and veteran status. All of these individual rivers then connect and flow into your organization. They form a powerful collective river to deal with complex challenges and generate new opportunities.

It's therefore advisable when recruiting to incorporate talent from as many sources as possible. For example, you can use Google's Programmable Search Engine (PSE) to narrow billions of indexed web pages down to sites and pages of interest such as LinkedIn profiles pages, Instagram bios, and Twitter bios for "social recruiting." You can surgically find diverse talent flowing through the *entire* web.[23]

The PSE is impressive. I was blown away when I set one up for searching LinkedIn profiles. I had the speed and scope of Google's search engine to explore the entirety of LinkedIn. I could engage a diverse talent river—including pockets of high-potentials who often go unnoticed—with exceptional accuracy. If you're interested in Google's PSE, then do an Internet search for "Recruiting with the Google Programmable Search Engine (PSE) | The Complete Guide."[24]

Once you increase your access to a diverse source of talent, you then need to ensure there is no biased and insensitive language in your job advertisements. For example, terms such as "aggressively pursue" regarding sales roles can signal to female applicants that men are more likely to be hired. Or, worse, the software architecture terminology "master/slave" in relation to database jobs could easily communicate that you're racially insensitive. By using this biased and insensitive language, you discourage or turn off highly capable people who would've added diverse and meaningful perspectives to your team—and who will instead enhance someone else's team.

Fortunately, there are emerging CLS-relevant solutions for breaking down these dams in your talent river, including natural language processing tools to automatically evaluate DEI language in job ads, as well as augmented writing platforms to provide real-time DEI guidance when crafting job descriptions. You can even use these tools to detect and develop a leader's ability to convey empathetic messages— for example, leaders receive automated prompts when writing job ads to ensure the tone is collaborative and supportive. As one founder put it, the technology is like "Grammarly for empathy."[25,26]

In addition to job advertisements, ineffective and biased candidate assessments can also lead to dams in your talent river. As I mentioned earlier, we know that extroverts are better at landing top jobs even though introverts tend to add more value, and leaders tend to select people they want rather than people they need, often subconsciously selecting people like themselves. This problem is then made worse through the use of totally meaningless tools such as the Myers-Briggs Type Indicator or catastrophically bad algorithms that exclude millions of capable applicants every year.[27,28]

CLS allows you to remove this dam with state-of-the-art solutions. For example, my cofounders and I at HR Machine created INQHIRE, a tool to match a candidate's real, not just stated, personality traits with a hiring agent's real needs, not just stated wants.[29]

The tool we developed is a three-step process for debiased hiring:

1. Multiple individuals on the hiring side (e.g., demographically diverse supervisors, peers, and subordinates) use our tool to create a 360° personality profile of the ideal candidate; this removes the biased preference of any single hiring agent or recruiter.

2. The tool then requires applicants to repeatedly choose between pairs of statements that best describe their personality— a statement related to extraversion versus a statement related to openness, then an extraversion statement versus a statement about honesty, and so on. This "forced choice" design prevents the candidates from simply rating themselves high on a desirable trait such as extraversion. It's about relative differences. They have to make subtle trade-offs about aspects of their personality, and this generates an accurate picture of their overall profile.

3. Our platform then increases interview intelligence. We incorporate individual test results with behavioral science to automatically generate interview questions tailored to the candidate's specific strengths and opportunities for improvement.

Collectively, these three steps produce a debiased bull's-eye of the ideal profile, an accurate assessment of how close a candidate's traits are to the target profile, and a reliable interview process for gauging an applicant's ability to perform and grow in the organization.

Leaders who combine these advancements in hiring technology with solutions for creating DEI-sensitive language in the early stages of recruitment are going to achieve next-level results with unmatched human capital. You'll be able to attract many tributaries of talent that you can turn into one highly competitive river flowing into your organization.

Challenge: Human and Social Capital Utilization and Inclusive Behavior

The next step is demonstrating concern for progress to boost trust among stakeholders. Simple visualizations, for example, surface DEI opportunities for improvement, and they send a clear message that you're paying attention. The City of Chicago's Office of Equity and Racial Justice, for instance, developed a comprehensive publicly available dashboard for demonstrating its ongoing commitment to employment diversity and areas in need of improvement. And MIT has a campus diversity dashboard to explore the gender, race, and ethnicity of its community. Such dashboards add value by providing transparency and insight into diversity trends. They are a great tool for displaying your authentic commitment to DEI.[30,31,32]

However, diversity dashboards are just the start for CLS-driven leaders. An increasingly sophisticated approach for understanding trends in DEI is combining network analysis with natural language processing. Now that communication and collaboration platforms such as Slack and Microsoft Teams are increasingly common in organizations, leaders can "passively" analyze the tone of conversations and explore who is working with whom to assess levels of exclusionary language and behavior. You may find that explicitly everyone has learned to use DEI friendly language (e.g., avoiding the term *man-hours*). However, through the use of network analysis, you may also identify implicit behavior where individuals are systematically excluded from important, promotion-relevant opportunities such as meetings with key decision-makers.

As Deloitte states, organizational network analysis, "can serve as a useful method to measure inclusion—uncovering quantifiable inequities in collaboration and mentorship, among other relationships, that reveal a critical need for focused efforts to promote equity and foster belonging." If leaders don't take advantage of CLS-driven tech to avoid this say-do gap, then they will end up reinforcing a façade of inclusivity while remaining incapable of extracting the full value of DEI.[33]

To start driving next-level DEI, you need to look at the data with your team being honest about any discrepancies between words and deeds. As a CLS-driven leader, you need to constantly focus on the data and incorporate experts to confirm or reject the presence of any implicit DEI problems in your organization.

If say-do gaps are your professional reality, then you must dig deeper into the underlying mechanisms of DEI and the corresponding data you can extract from your organization. The likelihood of bridging the gap between talking DEI and living DEI is extremely low unless you properly tap into your available resources. This is why the next evolution of CLS tech is moving toward relationship intelligence. For example, another team I'm a part of at HSC Analytics uses emerging tech to map, navigate, and engage employees.[34]

We first visually map an entire organization's human and social capital network—these are the individuals and their relationships. This step establishes who knows what and who's working with whom on what. It allows you to identify the silos that emerge due to human biases, such as a preference for colleagues with similar cultural backgrounds.

Next, to help break down silos, we implement a navigation function that looks and feels similar to Google Maps—it's like Google Maps for organizational networks. This tool allows you to navigate your professional network to find diverse mentors, colleagues, and teams. It's a digital networking assistant navigating a path from your trusted contacts to their trusted contacts and so on until you reach the people and resource you need to develop and grow.

Finally, the engage feature of our platform is for building diverse teams and communities. The tool can help you automatically match the right people with the right job regardless of traditional boundaries and biased silos. This is an opportunity for you to leverage diverse talent across your entire organization.[35]

The challenge once you have this level of connectivity is figuring out how to maximize its power. This is where advancements in collective intelligence come into play.

Challenge: Diverse and Collective Decision-Making

Research has shown that increasing opportunities for collective decision-making decreases the equity and inclusion problems associated with DEI. Emerging technology, such as "digital swarm intelligence," can help facilitate this collective transformation. Digital swarms are platforms designed to amplify real-time collective decision-making to answer questions, make predictions, reach decisions, and take actions with greater accuracy and group satisfaction.

An interesting example is Unanimous AI's "Swarm AI" technology. Stakeholders networked together with desktops or mobile devices are presented with multiple choices arranged in a circle on their individual screens. These choices can be about anything from teams most likely to win the Super Bowl to decisions about new products to develop. The users then repeatedly swipe toward their preferred alternative, and the underlying AI "swarms" to a collective choice based on factors such as the intensity and frequency of swipes. The beauty of this decision-making platform is that it isn't based on biased factors such as gender, ethnicity, or socioeconomic background. Everyone has an equal and inclusive chance to influence outcomes.[36]

In one such case with the Center for Intelligent Imaging at the University of California, San Francisco, the platform was utilized by radiologists for the complex challenge of interpreting knee MRIs—a task where there is often disagreement among experts. Their goal was to boost human swarm intelligence by (a) increasing consensus and (b) reducing biases, which often limit the decision-making power to a handful of highly ranked (and homogeneous) individuals while limiting the input of lower ranked yet capable practitioners. The outcome, flying in the face of years of tradition, was a clear win for the collective intelligence platform in accuracy relative to both highly ranked experts and AI-driven interpretations.[37]

Applying this tech could revolutionize the pace and quality of decision-making in organizations. It also represents an unprecedented opportunity to take inclusivity to the next level. Even if employees don't necessarily get their preferred outcome, everyone will (literally) have a hand in the decision-making process. Establishing this degree of engagement is what is takes to release the DEI talent river.

The key takeaway is that diverse, equitable, and inclusive input is powerful. And CLS facilitates decision making at scale: it puts an undeniable spotlight on DEI's importance, it unlocks new opportunities for leaders, and it liberates organizations from the tyranny of bias.

Let's now have a quick look at how JPMorgan Chase is using CLS to drive world-leading DEI initiatives.

DIVERSITY, EQUITY, AND INCLUSION Q&A WITH JPMORGAN CHASE

"With a clear and well-articulated DEI strategy, you can feel that the organization is well positioned to deliver sustainable change."
   —*Cecil Peters, Executive Director and EMEA Head of DEI, Head of Advancing Black Pathways, JPMorgan Chase*

For my Q&A session on DEI, I was fortunate enough to speak with Cecil Peters, Executive Director and EMEA Head of DEI as well as EMEA Head of Advancing Black Pathways at JPMorgan Chase.

JPMorgan Chase & Co. is a US-based multinational investment bank and financial services holding company with more than 270,000 employees worldwide. Its size and global reach makes the company diverse by nature, and its DEI mission statement reflects this awareness: "JPMorgan Chase is working to drive a diverse and inclusive culture for our employees and our business. Everything has to start at home—leaving no stone unturned, we're looking at our diverse recruiting practices, training, our products and services, and supplier diversity."

Given its inherent diversity, JPMorgan Chase is an ideal company with which to explore DEI. The following is what Mr. Peters had to say about the company's present and future initiatives.

Q: What DEI challenge or opportunity is of most interest to your organization?

A: There are multiple challenges across all demographics. With a clear and well-articulated DEI strategy, you can feel that the organization is well positioned to deliver sustainable change. However, ensuring that the leadership of the organization is inclusive presents the greatest challenge and opportunity. Many organizations have goals for leadership diversity, but much of the ability to influence the culture of an organization is held by team leaders and middle managers who may not have defined accountability or a measurement for success.

Q: What specific question(s) do you have regarding your organization's ability to address DEI?

A: None, as the DEI strategy is clearly articulated with an accountability framework for senior leaders.

Q: What specific expectations do you have about what's influencing your organization's ability to address DEI?

A: The biggest influence on our expectations is our CEO, who has stated quite unequivocally that everyone should feel that they belong, that he expects diversity to exist throughout all levels of the organization, and that leadership makes it very clear what the company stands for and what our values are.

Q: What data and tech are you using to address DEI?

A: We measure multiple demographics through asking people to self-identify. This is an optional request, but the more complete the information, the better equipped the organization is to develop meaningful opportunities for all demographics. We use standard third-party human capital management solutions along with internal data analytics reporting to create visibility on aggregated DEI metrics for those with the requisite access.

We are also investigating tooling to help manage the multiple employee resource groups (ERGs) that we have. With 275,000 employees worldwide, the ability to empower the leads of those ERGs to communicate with their communities and measure their progress is an evolution on our current position.

Q: What drove your data and tech choices (e.g., personal decision, team decision, data scientist decision, using what's available, some sort of systematic process for selecting data and tech)?

A: These are strategic HR solutions. DEI is a recipient of the product choice.

Q: What sort of data and/or tech are you using to track the impact of your DEI initiatives over time?

A: We set KPIs for all of our DEI areas of impact. These are tracked by each demographic to ensure that our investments match our priorities. This approach allows us to speak explicitly about the impact we have on our clients, communities, and employees.

We also speak of DEI being run as a business. Therefore, we have a finance department tracking all spending and a program office tracking success against the predefined DEI KPIs. We are also audited to validate that our processes support our strategy.

Q. What sort of data and/or tech are you using to track the impact of your DEI initiatives at multiple levels?

A: A large amount of data is monthly or quarterly scorecards, with narratives provided by the DEI leaders to their specific customer base. Scorecards are a combination of automated online reports and manually produced extracted reports. It is important that the narrative clearly gives direction on where the organization needs to focus and what tools are in place to help that change.

Q: What is the (expected) outcome of your tech-enabled plans for DEI?

A: We expect our tech enablement to cover all demographics more completely in all locations. For example, ethnicity self-identify data is not available in every country, but where it is we should seek to have our technology solutions encompass those countries.

Concluding Thoughts about My Interview with Cecil Peters

I see accountability, community building, prudent yet profound use of data, and a clear focus on CLS-driven growth as key pathways for DEI at JPMorgan Chase. Accountability comes from the top down, and a definitive framework is in place for senior leaders. As anyone working in digital transformation will tell you, having this high-level buy-in is a must for effective change.

In a company as large and diverse as JPMorgan Chase, the use of employee resource groups based on factors such as ethnicity, sexual orientation, and veteran status is an excellent way to build inclusive and supportive communities within and across regions. It'll be interesting to see how employee groups evolve as digital innovations improve connectivity within and between these networks. Instantly finding anyone anywhere in an organization will empower employees like never before.

Another insightful concept is the company's use of KPIs and running DEI as a business to ensure it is neither overspending on "all hype, no help" solutions nor underinvesting in DEI data and tech. I also see a consistent narrative of not basking in the glory of their current recognitions and accomplishments. The company is constantly innovating and assessing solutions to increase performance. CLS-driven leaders with this sense of mission and purpose will revolutionize DEI in business and society. It will fully release its DEI talent river.

CHAPTER 3

Breaking the Death-by-Meetings Curse and Other Engagement Killers

Employee engagement—also referred to as work engagement—is another important factor in leadership driven by computational leadership science (CLS). A highly engaged workforce promotes organizational well-being and next-level performance, whereas a disengaged workforce leads to negative spiraling where employees detach, relationships break down and dissolve, people leave as soon as they can, and organizational goals suffer.

This toxic trend is perhaps why companies spend more than $100B annually on engagement initiatives and why attention to retaining an engaged workforce is increasing. PwC recently found that hiring and retention is the number one concern among business leaders, while Gartner found that workforce issues such as engagement rose 32% in importance from 2021 to 2022 to grab the number three spot on its top ten list of CEO priorities—just behind growth (number one) and tech-related transformation (number two).[1,2]

Top management is prioritizing and investing so heavily in engagement because an engaged workforce significantly outperforms a disengaged workforce on almost every measure of performance. Gallup's extensive meta-analytic review of "the relationship between engagement at work and organizational outcomes" finds that highly engaged organizations—relative to disengaged groups—score:

- 23% higher in profitability;
- 18% higher in productivity (sales);

- 10% higher on customer loyalty and engagement;

- 64% higher in workplace safety;

- 58% higher in patient safety (mortality and falls);

- 41% higher in quality (defects);

- 66% higher in well-being (thriving employees); and

- 13% higher in organizational citizenship behavior (participation).

If that's not enough proof, these highly engaged organizations also score:

- 81% lower in absenteeism;

- 28% lower in shrinkage (theft); and

- 18%–43% lower in turnover depending on the sector.[3]

And if you're still not convinced regarding the value of a highly engaged workforce, a small army of scientists are finding the same results as the big consultancies. An engaged workforce corresponds to task performance and client satisfaction. Engagement is also a good predictor of innovative and entrepreneurial behavior, helping behavior, increased team performance, future wages, and occupational ranking.[4,5,6,7,8,9]

Research has also discovered compelling ironies in the world of engagement. Those tasked with building an engaged workforce— managers—frequently report some of the lowest levels of engagement. And those who reported some of the lowest levels of engagement before COVID-19—employees who work exclusively remote or hybrid—now tend to have some of the highest levels of engagement.[10]

Such ironic shifts in engagement and the structural problems in who's suffering the most with disengagement says a lot about our ability to drive change. On one hand, we have mountains of information regarding the value of engagement, yet on the other hand, we have limited knowledge on how to increase and sustain this critical factor for performance and growth. To address this shortcoming, our next adventure in the CLS journey explores what we know about the composition of engagement, what we don't know about the mechanics of engagement, and how CLS-relevant technology can help you achieve next-level results. Finally, I share a recent interview I had with senior leadership in Workforce Analytics at Merck & Co. regarding its approach to engagement and employee experience.

WHAT WE KNOW ABOUT ENGAGEMENT AND LEADERSHIP

Gallup, a thought leader in the field, defines *employee engagement* as a sense of enthusiasm and involvement in one's work and workplace. Those who are engaged display high levels of energy and are much more immersed in their work relative to those who are there for the paycheck. Similarly, in the academic literature, *engagement* is often referred to as "a positive, fulfilling, affective-motivational state of work-related well-being that is characterized by vigor, dedication, and absorption."[11,12]

Engagement is broadly broken down into person-centered and situation-centered concerns. The person side focuses on employee traits such as personality. Initial research, for instance, suggests conscientious and extraverted individuals are generally more engaged. On the situation-centered side of engagement, scholars and practitioners explore how vigor, dedication, and absorption in work fluctuate as a function of job demands (e.g., death by meetings), available resources (e.g., mentors), and proactive behavior (e.g., networking).[13]

Challenging Job Demands and Hindering Job Demands

The situation-centered side makes up the majority of what we know and focuses primarily on two basic types of job demands: challenging job demands and hindering job demands. Challenging job demands are those demands providing opportunities for personal and professional growth such as the sense of personal growth experienced when time pressure unleashes hidden levels of effort or increased responsibility leads to growth as a leader. Hindering challenges, on the other hand, are situational demands detracting from opportunities for growth and goal attainment. These are costly investments often involving ambiguous, conflicting, or useless tasks such as unproductive meetings to tick boxes.

Challenging job demands—relative to hindering job demands— typically contribute to engagement when people have the necessary resources to achieve personal and professional goals. For example, taking on additional responsibility is an excellent growth opportunity for budding leaders, provided they have resources such as mentors and a network of peers to support them on their journey. Otherwise, this beneficial challenging job demand will turn into a hindrance where the role is ambiguous and stressful. The outcome is a disengage employee who's more likely to leave than to lead.

Personal Resources and Job Resources

In order to leverage the power of challenging job demands and engagement, you need to understand your available resources and how to dynamically calibrate them according to the person and the situation. Resources at your disposal are divided into two segments: personal resources and job resources. Personal resources relate to an individual's sense of control over their environment. Factors connected to this type of resources include optimism, self-esteem, and self-efficacy. As a leader, you can improve these factors by providing your people with opportunities to master new things in a safe space or allowing them to decide how they get their work done as long as it gets done.

Job resources—the single most important antecedent of engagement—can be physical, psychological, social, or organizational, spanning from basic equipment and supplies to social support from the employer. Job resources intrinsically motivate when they address deep-seated needs for competence (e.g., training and development), autonomy (e.g., reduced bureaucracy), and relatedness (e.g., a strong support network). Job resources also extrinsically motivate employees because they help with factors such as salary and promotion.[14]

Job resources take the top spot as an influencer of employee engagement because they (a) decrease the negative effect of hindering demands such as tedious meetings, (b) increase the positive effect of challenging demands such as taking on promotion-relevant tasks, and (c) provide the greatest opportunity for your people to learn and grow. To put it simply, you have the best chance of maximizing engagement when challenging demands are introduced, hindering demands are reduced, and a sufficient amount of job and personal resources are available.

The Reality of Engagement

Though introducing challenging opportunities, removing detrimental obstacles, and providing people with the resources they need to succeed seems like an easy enough task for leaders, mounting evidence suggests organizations are failing. Gallup found that employees reported significant drops in crucial elements of engagement from 2021 to 2022. Employees reported declines in clarity of expectations, necessary materials and equipment, reduced autonomy to "do what they do best," and a diminished sense of connection to the organization's mission and purpose.[15]

The current work environment, in short, is a toxic combination of hindering job demands, a deficit of basic resources such as equipment and materials, and unmet implicit needs such as autonomy and relatedness to others. All the while, society is going through a fundamental upheaval in how people work and what they're willing to do for a paycheck.

It's no wonder the Great Resignation developed out of the pandemic. Practitioners and researchers are completely missing key pieces of the puzzle regarding the dynamics of engagement. They require adaptive tools to address changing needs over time. Unfortunately, there's currently nothing in the market that can enable organizations to monitor employee-specific obstacles in real time and provide tailored resources—so those employees can overcome hurdles and take on new engagement-increasing challenges. Organizations traditionally rely on management to accomplish this task—but, given that managers are already stretched to the limit with a variety of demands and the fact that most employees think their managers are part of the problem, things aren't likely to change unless leaders decide to leverage innovative data and technology.[16,17]

To deal with this unacceptable problem, let's now turn our attention to mapping out the blind spots in engagement research and practice. Then we'll focus on laying the groundwork for CLS-driven solutions.

WHAT WE DON'T KNOW ABOUT ENGAGEMENT

To start discussing what we don't know regarding engagement, here's one final thing we do know: The majority of existing research is based on (a) between-person comparisons of engagement, and (b) thin-sliced, moment-in-time surveys capturing a static picture of engagement. The outcome is a very limited perspective of reality. Between-person comparisons means we don't know much about how engagement changes within a person. Take a moment and think about that. Likewise, a survey will help you understand *what* is happening at any given moment (e.g., a momentary high or low in engagement between individuals or groups), but you cannot reliably know how, why, where, or when engagement changed over time. You have fuzzy shadows of the past rather than a real-time granular data stream of present needs for future results. Simply put, we know very little about the dynamics of engagement.

This void in our understanding makes it impossible to tailor engagement strategies to individuals or groups. We don't know *how* their personal needs manifest, *why* certain interventions work for them, *where* particular attention is required for their continued engagement, or *when* their tailored strategies require updating. The following are three major unknowns restricting employee engagement.

Unknown Engagement Dynamics

Complex dynamics of engagement remain in the shadows because most of the prevailing tools lack scope. I cannot emphasize enough how much we do not know about fluctuating patterns of engagement within-person across time and situation. For example, it's unclear how newcomer engagement evolves within the first year—a critical time for employee retention—nor how factors such as onboarding and mentorships create and maintain engagement throughout the first year and beyond. Similarly, we do not systematically understand what influences engagement in specific demographic groups, different sectors, or occupations. There are some glimmers of understanding about personal fluctuations, but a (near) real-time method for monitoring individual-level engagement and developing tailored interventions are necessary if you want to take your leadership to the next level. You need a CLS-relevant system to map specific job demands and necessary resources for each individual. In doing so, you are able to create bespoke, continually updating interventions for a highly—and dare I say it—fully engaged workforce.[18,19,20]

Unknown Engagement HR Functions

We also don't understand how to systematically foster high levels of engagement. For example, we know relatively little about the role HR systems can play in increasing engagement. Research has provided some insights regarding the influence of structural resources such as ample opportunities for professional development, but truly understanding the mechanics of engagement over time remains elusive. Experts can't even agree on how engagement spreads throughout an organization, so it's not surprising the finer points are murky. Organizational systems, therefore, need to move beyond traditional administrative tasks such as the ubiquitous annual survey and instead deeply embed engagement monitoring from recruitment to ongoing training and development to retirees as mentors. This is where CLS using advancements in science and technology to track, analyze, and drive engagement in real time will play an important role in maximizing your organization's ability to create a vibrant and game-changing workforce.[21,22]

Unknown Engagement Leadership Factors

Finally, and most relevant to the theme of this book, our knowledge regarding the impact of leadership on engagement is topical at best.

There's some work looking at concepts such as the positive effects of transformational leadership, but the overall foundation is weak. Little is known about the leadership process for facilitating the spread of engagement. To overcome this problem, experts are calling for more attention on informal, distributed, and shared leadership. Incorporating these more adaptive, less formal leadership styles will add to the known value of transformational leadership and increase your ability to promote engagement.[23,24,25]

Leadership also tends to take an intuitive, trial-and-error approach to understanding and guiding engagement efforts. This can lead to many misapplications of what we know. For example, increasing work challenges and time constraints across your organization might feel like a natural way to stretch your staff and get the best out of people, but without sufficient resources and the removal of hindering job demands, engagement initiatives can quickly turn into burnout initiatives. This is an extremely dangerous blind spot considering the number of restrictive barriers top management teams can introduce—especially during times of crisis to maintain control.[26]

CLS-DRIVEN ENGAGEMENT LEADERSHIP

As a CLS-minded leader, going beyond intuition is your opportunity to identify the symptoms of disengagement and treat the cause like never before. In this section we'll combine data, science, and tech to prevent death by meetings and other engagement killers.

Challenge: Understanding the Fluctuating Dynamics of Engagement

Capturing (near) real-time changes in employee engagement—down to the individual level—represents a monumental shift in science and practice. It's a space where siloed value connects and multiplies. Practitioners, for example, know from experience that methods for measuring employee engagement need to be short, sweet, and actionable; otherwise, nobody buys in. Behavioral scientists, on the other hand, know that methods for measuring engagement need to touch on psychologically relevant factors such as challenging and hindering job demands; otherwise, the insights are not effective. And CLS-driven leaders know how to administer this cocktail of practice and research to achieve and maintain high levels of engagement.

Fortunately, there are several technologies for taking you to this next level. You can deploy short and frequent pulse survey using open-ended questions infused with natural language processing to gain a better understanding of (a) the primary topics associated with engagement in your organization (e.g., concerns about access to certain job resources), and (b) how your employees feel about your ability to address their concerns. This form of automated *topic modeling* and *sentiment analysis* allows you to frequently assess what is needed and then surgically adjust your approach across the entire organization. Asking your employees simple and scientific questions such as, "What resources do you need to do your job and grow?" and "What barriers do you need removed to do your job and grow?" in an open-ended fashion *at scale* provides them with an immediate sense of engagement, and then acting on these suggestions—potentially tailored to each employee—takes your effectiveness to a level most only dream about.

Your emerging tools for tracking granular shifts in engagement also opens the door for better staff recognition and praise. According to a Gallup survey, only one in three employees strongly agreed they received recognition and praise for their achievements in the past seven years. Too often everyone gets so caught up in spreadsheets, meetings, and just getting through the day that the basic needs for gratitude and appreciation fade into the background. For example, great leaders shielding employees from the top-down sludge of bureaucracy receive little attention, and great employees quietly mentoring newcomers and promoting engagement frequently go unnoticed.[27]

You can rectify this lack of real-time praise by incorporating employee recognition software. There are several platforms to choose from with a variety of features from quick informal praise to formal rewards such as Amazon products, gift cards, and donation options. Though this technology is not a cure-all, it can help you surface the good and praise it. Just make sure the software you choose has features to help these praiseworthy employees grow. Rewarding people with paid opportunities to earn micro-credentials or a few days to explore other parts of the organization is far more engaging than the gift of a fleece with a corporate logo. You need to creatively tap into the implicit motivators of engagement—competence, autonomy, and relatedness—not just swag and thumbs up icons.[28]

Challenge: Understanding the Structural Pillars of Engagement

In addition to the dynamics of engagement, you should also consider how the structural aspects of your organization are influencing an employee's dedication to their work. A major opportunity for establishing elevated levels of engagement is supporting employees throughout their journey—from job applicant to their exit and beyond. There are several ways CLS-driven leaders can use digital tools to support this evolving process of growth. The following are four examples to kickstart your transformation.

CLS LEADERS REMOVE BARRIERS AND INCREASE ENGAGEMENT EARLY AND OFTEN. Engagement needs to happen before day one of an employee's journey and continue throughout their entire progression. CLS-driven leaders remove frustrating, pointless, and dangerous selection methods in the recruitment and hiring phase. As mentioned in the previous chapter on DEI, totally meaningless assessment tools such as the Myers-Briggs Type Indicator (MBTI) or flawed algorithms incorrectly rejecting millions of viable job candidates are continually utilized. This is a huge hindrance as candidates flow through a cumbersome process on their path to employment. Simply put, frustrated candidates turn into frustrated new hires—provided they accept the offer at all—and frustrated new hires frequently turn into frustrated ex-employees.[29,30]

Breaking down these initial barriers requires next-generation platforms, not archaic tools such as the MBTI or biased first-gen algorithms that alienate people. Emerging AI-driven platforms are rapidly going beyond old-school ways of doing business. AI-powered applicant tracking systems are increasingly effective at identifying high-potential applicants and quickly engaging them. A readily available technology to help with the application process, for instance, are chatbots using conversational AI. Research shows that most people prefer the quick and direct Q&A responses chatbots can provide to simple questions. These platforms can also establish early-stage engagement with hyper-personalized emails to candidates at scale. They automatically generate outbound messages tailored to everyone's background, experience, and unique candidate-role fit. By incorporating this CLS-relevant tech into your daily leadership practices, you no longer need to send unengaging boilerplate messages or waste vast amounts of time personalizing emails. Instead, you can maintain early-stage engagement as you funnel in talent.[31,32]

The benefits of this CLS-driven approach include a significant improvement in (AI-assisted) candidate filtering, noticeable cost savings by automating parts of the application process such as pre-interview testing, and a better candidate experience by getting back to—and hiring—qualified individuals faster. The result is a supported candidate who will transform into a highly engaged new hire.

CLS LEADERS MAINTAIN POSITIVE MOMENTUM THROUGHOUT THE ONBOARDING PROCESS. Effective onboarding is essential for taking full advantage of your CLS-inspired talent river. Scholars and practitioners consistently find positive outcomes such as increased job satisfaction, greater productivity, and significant boosts in employee retention relative to organizations with poor onboarding practices. The Society for Human Resource Management found that 69% of employees are more likely to stay with an organization for three years if the onboarding is engaging while another study found that new hire retention improved by 82%.[33,34,35]

CLS helps leaders capitalize on this retention opportunity. For example, you can use an AI-supported platform to rapidly match mentors with mentees at scale. This tool finds the best fit between mentor qualifications and mentee needs. It also nudges the duo to maintain regular conversations, provides them with key points to discuss so they stay on track, and allows the mentee to provide feedback after each meeting so the mentor can assess their ability to add value. This is a prime example of how CLS-inspired technology turbocharges a structured onboarding process, provides new hires with valuable job resources, and consequently takes your engagement skills to the next level.[36,37]

CLS LEADERS KEEP THINGS CONTINUOUSLY ENGAGING. Another major structural concern is the transition from establishing engagement in newcomers to maintaining engagement over time. Here, you can introduce structural changes such as the introduction of gamification tech to make the environment more playful and learning platforms to enrich the environment with opportunities for increasing competence and a sense of autonomy.

Gamification of work is the use of game techniques—points, levels, badges, and competition—to motivate and engage employees. Features range from simple progress bars and leaderboards in sales situations to extremely complex platforms for managing simulated global supply chains or organization-wide operations during a crisis. You can then combine gamification with learning tech to introduce an extremely powerful tool for engagement and growth: "gamified learning."

An interesting example of gamified learning is the Deloitte Leadership Academy. The professional services firm embedded missions, badges, leadership boards, rewards, and other gamified elements into the learning process to increase user engagement and motivation to complete necessary training. It was an immediate success with participants displaying "almost addictive behavior."[38] Another example is ExxonMobil's use of VR for safety training. The platform transports users into a 3D environment filled with gamified elements such as increasing challenges, strategy, surprise, payoff, and visual appeal. The outcome is a far more engaging learning experience relative to traditional safety training methods. Think of it like an immersive choose-your-own-adventure book for learning mission-critical information as a team. It's highly effective and versatile. Settings to apply gamified learning include customer service, health care, sales, construction and manufacturing, and emergency services.[39]

CLS LEADERS DRIVE CONNECTIVITY. A requirement at every stage in the journey is ensuring employees can rapidly access all the people, teams, and other resources your organization has to offer. This is why my cofounders and I started HSC Analytics—short for Human and Social Analytics. We're working on a network mapping platform so individuals can plot a course to the resources they need to succeed (see Chapter 2 for a description of our work). Such tech helps everyone from senior managers needing to quickly find and wrap individuals around tendering opportunities to employees looking for new challenges better aligned with their competencies to newcomers building their network in the age of 100% remote working.[40]

CLS-driven leaders using digital tools to increase connectivity see opportunity where others might see risk. Society's abrupt shift to remote working, for example, may cause some leaders to introduce excessive employee monitoring systems only to find that trust—and subsequently engagement—tanks. CLS-driven leaders won't do that. They'll avoid the slippery slope of control by embracing what we know from research—specifically, providing access to necessary resources and promoting a sense of competence, autonomy, and relatedness increases engagement, *not* monitoring. And they'll transform virtual environments into fruitful spaces for next-level connectivity and growth. These leaders will reduce dissatisfaction while increasing trust, commitment, and other outcomes indicative of great leadership.

Challenge: Understanding the Death-by-Meetings Curse

Now, for an added bonus, I'll briefly touch on an emerging CLS method for reducing one of the most disengaging factors of all time: never-ending meetings.

Companies can increase key drivers of engagement such as autonomy and boost productivity—up to 73% in some cases—by banning meetings up to three days per week. And one way you can reduce meetings is streamlining collaboration with blockchain. As this technology matures and spreads, it has the potential to reduce the number of meetings for everything from international collaborations to small product teams.[41,42]

Blockchain allows many individuals to share information securely and transparently across all parties. Everyone has access to the same standardized set of information in one place, which is easily trackable and nearly impossible to change without permission. Blockchain also ensures everyone hits their targets through the use of timestamps and "smart contracts"—which only implement predetermined agreements and disperse resources once parties meet specific conditions along the digital path.

Blockchain can work to automate time-consuming and disengaging tasks such as running constant status update meetings. For example, timestamps could significantly reduce "I did this," "I didn't do that" emails and meetings because every action is securely logged for all parties to review. It can also eliminate the need to give manual permission to advance every step of a project. For example, a smart contract can eliminate "yes you can," "no you can't" emails and meetings during a large project because teams only progress once they hit their targets and unlock the next section of an agreement.

These shared digital ledgers can also help leaders manage complex collaborations with multiple internal and external parties who tend to keep their own records. Also, if you want to be extra clever, you can embed the recognition and reward systems mentioned earlier into your blockchain to continually acknowledge people for hitting targets along the way.

Combining these advancements in blockchain with what we know from research and practice is yet another example of why CLS is so powerful. Science tells us hindering job demands—those taking you away from the tasks you need to succeed—are hugely detrimental, and in practice we know meetings are one of the main culprits. Blockchain technology is turning this knowledge into solutions for preventing death by meetings. Leaders using this tech to remove hindrances will provide their people with the most important resource around—time.

To see this digital revolution in practice, let's take a look at how one of the best in the business is listening to its employees and transforming that information into high performance.

Employee Engagement Q&A with Merck & Co.

"One way we approach employee experience is taking immediate, incremental action based on data-informed insights and explicitly tying the action to the insight, especially when it's feedback from employees. . . ."
—*Dr. Lauren Boyatzi, Associate Director and Head of Employee Listening, Workforce Analytics at Merck & Co.*

I had the wonderful opportunity to sit down with Dr. Lauren Boyatzi, Associate Director and Head of Employee Listening in Workforce Analytics at Merck & Co.

Merck & Co. is a global pharmaceutical company with over 68,000 employees. The company's culture and values, as stated on its website, are based on "a culture that embraces scientific excellence, operates with the highest standards of integrity, expands access to our products, and employs a diverse workforce that values collaboration." Given this emphasis on building and maintaining collaborative work environments in such a large company, Merck makes for an excellent example of how organizations can use CLS-driven data and tech to encourage industry-leading engagement.

The first point Dr. Boyatzi emphasized is that engagement is part of Merck's overall focus on "employee experience"—that is, the experience that employees go through from hire to exit. It's not only related to the job but also to the overall environment, touchpoints, and the employee's perception from beginning to end (i.e., what an employee thinks, feels, and sees).

Accordingly, I'll stick with Merck's preferred terminology during the Q&A, but keep in mind that its impactful initiatives broadly apply to engagement efforts if that's your specific topic of interest.

Q: What employee experience challenge or opportunity is of most interest to your organization?

A: Given our industry and focus, our ability to attract, retain, and engage top scientific talent as well as the teams that will allow us to save and improve lives is critical to success. We have a laser focus on talent attraction for that purpose, but we're also very engaged in career development, retention, employee value, and bringing the "future of work" to the forefront today. As an example, we've launched a formal "gig work" service where employees can apply for temporary assignments in areas they'd like to learn more about. Diversity and inclusion are also key to how we operate, how we engage employees, and how we drive competitive advantage. Our focus on D&I relates to everything from our employee base to our suppliers to our clinical trials, and we've created a data-driven link on how D&I creates success for us.

Q: What specific question(s) do you have regarding your organization's ability to address employee experience?

A: The root of our questions we tend to explore are based on trying to understand what employees value (which is different based on the role), and then understanding how well the company enables them to do great work and contribute to our mission. We're a big company, so executing well on organizing the many employee experience projects we invest in is a focus. We're very deep into understanding the behaviors, attitudes, and habits that support our culture—both now and for the future. We also spend a great deal of time researching diversity and inclusion trends (e.g., moving to ESG, psychological safety, and individual dimensions to understand employees' perspectives and needs). In fact, Merck was a cofounder of the "OneTen" initiative in the US, which supports these aims.[43]

Q: What specific expectations do you have about what's influencing your organization's ability to address employee experience?

The first thing influencing Merck's ability to address employee experience is ownership and clarifying decision rights. Guiding effective employee experience initiatives requires desire from all managerial layers, from the top down, to emphasize the importance of employee experience as well as a desire for implementation and improvement. To implement and improve, we also focus on specific organizational capabilities such as leadership, an employee-oriented culture, and systems to refine our practices. Doing all this requires us to focus on big influential factors such as overall company culture and an appetite for change as well as organizational diagnostic capabilities to identify influential issues. Finally, we also consider common influential factors for any initiative such as bureaucracy, time, and resources.

Q: What sort of information led you to these expectations (e.g., professional journals, expert advice, experience, intuition)?

A: We tend to learn from external experts (particularly peers who have been through similar scenarios) as well as the great thinking coming out of both the academic arena and the robust pipeline of data-driven research findings other companies are starting to release.

Q: What data and tech are you using to address employee experience?

A: We use several tools to first measure employee experience; then we use several tools to provide solutions, including employee listening tools (Microsoft's GLINT survey platform) as well as other Microsoft tools, Workday, and a robust data science platform for insight generation. We leverage other tools as appropriate for specific needs. What's important to us is not only the proper use of those tools but also availability of the insights at scale. In addition, we also use some traditional methods of listening intended to provide us with insights including engaging our Employee Business Resource Group members regarding their experience, conducting bold and inclusive conversations, listening circles, etc. Together, these form an in-depth quantitative and qualitative narrative for the organization.

Q: What drove your data and tech choices (e.g., personal decision, team decision, data scientist decision, using what's available, some sort of systematic process for selecting data and tech)?

A: It's a systematic process for selecting data and tech. There are a number of factors we consider when making our choices. For example, the speed of getting results back is important. Likewise, the tools integration and automation capability with HRIS. Another driving factor is scalability to (and usability for) HR business partners and managers across the company. We also select tech allowing us to turn self-service capabilities into advanced analysis such as using NLP to analyze comments in automated employee platforms. There's a strong systematic focus on ensuring our data and tech choices align with leadership aspirations around employee listening.

Q: What sort of data and/or tech are you using to track the impact of your employee experience initiatives over time?

A: We've had annual and biennial surveys measuring employee engagement and the employee experience for most of the past 15 years. We now employ a pulse survey strategy with shorter, more frequent touchpoints. The data includes responses to any actions the divisions took to improve employee engagement and experience. Most of these actions are taken (and measured) locally such as individual managers, specific organizations, and so on, and the results are put directly in managers' hands, providing them with the ability to accurately assess impact.

Q. What sort of data and/or tech are you using to track the impact of your employee experience at multiple levels?

A: We analyze our employee experience results with numerous attributes and with cross-sections of the population to better understand differences. Attributes and cross-sections include:

- Geography (region, country, location);
- Job level;
- Organization;
- Number of recognition rewards provided to employees; and
- Sales/non-sales.

Q: What sort of data and/or tech are you using to track DEI aspects of your employee experience initiatives?

A: Inclusion is a measure that is deeply embedded in our core metrics, and we even disclose some data externally through our ESG reports. We track trends on inclusion and belonging, and where it is permitted, we add in a lens of different constituencies across the company. These are rolled into executive dashboards, and some data is shared publicly.

Q: What is the (expected) outcome of your tech-enabled plans for employee experience?

A: One way we approach employee experience is taking immediate, incremental action based on data-informed insights and explicitly tying the action to the insight, especially when it's feedback from employees. We've adopted Workday to help create a more holistic process and have incorporated more services over time to create a desired, more seamless employee experience from hire to exit. End users will have a simple way to manage their work-life balance at the company—from onboarding through to career development. Finally, we encourage continuous improvement.

Concluding Thoughts about My Interview with Lauren Boyatzi

Merck & Co. epitomizes a sense of balance in its CLS-driven approach to employee engagement and experience. The company relies on a broad set of tools and data to effectively calibrate its needs and solutions, and it ensures immediate, yet incremental action based on data-informed insights. In other words, the company uses a variety of digital tools and implements them with thoughtful determination. Achieving and maintaining this digital balance between experimentation and consistency turbocharges the company's ability to create next-level employee engagement. It's the sweet spot for unleashing the full power of CLS.

CHAPTER **4**

Mastering the Bubbles and Tightropes of Sustainability

While I was writing this chapter, the phrase "something's gotta give" kept repeating in my mind. It's a simple concept. If business and society prioritize short-term self-interest over long-term group interest, then something's gotta give.

This isn't about the Johnny Mercer song "Something's Gotta Give." It's an undeniable truth that humanity will suffer if we don't align individual and group interests. I recall, for example, an oceanography professor who told me, many years before Hurricane Katrina, about the pending threat to New Orleans and what needed to be done to avoid catastrophe. Unfortunately, we know how that played out. The city sustained billions of dollars in property damage and suffered a significant loss of life because decision-makers wanted to save millions of dollars in flood wall design. Then, in the midst of recovering from Katrina, the world was rocked by the 2007–2008 financial crisis. Here, again, short-term, self-interested practices—in this case, predatory lending and excessive financial risk-taking—significantly damaged the long-term sustainability of society as a whole.[1,2]

Now, moving to the present day, let's look at how COVID-19 came into being. Hyper-urbanization, though economically beneficial in the short term, is known to increase the risk of contagious disease in the long term. The increasing proximity of certain animals to humans— arguably driven by the benefits of short-term, industrial-scale wildlife farming—led the SARS-CoV-2 virus to transfer from (likely) bats to humans. From there it spread rapidly because unsustainably high levels of global travel fueled "stealth transmission" before we were able to take preventative lockdown measures. Finally, humans' vulnerability to the virus mixing with unsustainable limits on health care capacity led to significant loss of life. COVID-19, in short, will go down in history as a series of unstainable ticking time bombs—one triggered after the next—that resulted in the biggest disruption to business and society in generations.[3,4,5,6,7,8,9]

What does this say about the future? What other unsustainable time bombs are lurking around the corner? Europe is suffering from war and dealing with astronomical energy prices due to an unsustainable relationship with Russia. The food industry continues to profit from the excessive use of additives such as sugar even though that contributes to shocking levels of diabetes and obesity—which equates to crushing health care costs for both employers and employees. Venture capitalists profit from driving the rapid growth of start-ups even though that's creating a huge, debt-ridden bubble. And let's not get started on the next looming financial crisis building up like a dark scourge from the bowels of Mordor.[10,11]

As the above examples make clear, leaders will need to guide business and society through an increasing number of challenges related to decades of unsustainable behavior. To do so successfully will call for correctly framing and answering one question above all else: Why is this happening? What is the *why* of sustainability? Then, and only then, can leaders determine *how* to bring about much-needed change.

This chapter will therefore explore a deeper perspective of sustainability. I will cover key steps for establishing "systemic sustainability" in your organization and share the computational leadership science (CLS) advantage for establishing sustainable growth. I will also identify the say-do gaps in business and society hindering progress. For example, sustainability can't thrive on green marketing over green doing. Instead, as will become clear, leaders driven by CLS have an unprecedented opportunity to maximize economic, environmental, and social values by incorporating accountability, honesty, and transparency into their leadership equation. Finally, in the Q&A section, I'll explore how Tony's Chocolonely—a best-in-class chocolate manufacturer— is pursuing this deep commitment to sustainability with world-leading business practices and innovative technology.

What Sustainability Is

Sustainability is the balance between self-interest and group interest across the full spectrum of ecological, economic, and social concerns—the so-called triple bottom line. Unfortunately, because there are so few examples of large-scale sustainability, the best way to understand the phenomenon is exploring examples of when systems are not working. For example, experts are aware of the food industry's role in obesity and diabetes and how the pressure for increasing shareholder value—often by selling unhealthy products—stresses a separate but connected health care system. As researchers pointed out over a decade ago in the *Journal of the American Medical Association*, "In a market-driven economy, [the food] industry tends to act opportunistically in the interests of maximizing profit. Problems arise when society fails to perceive this situation accurately."[12]

This struggle with sustainability is a tension that affects most sectors—such as energy, retail, tourism, and transportation—and challenges all layers of society, from individual consumers to interconnected, globalized enterprises and countries. In other words, sustainability's core principle of balancing egoistic and altruistic concerns applies to any dynamic where individual-level benefits bring about increasing group-level costs to the broader stakeholder community—for example, sugars economic value versus its threat to public health.

To rectify this imbalance, experts focus on sustainable development. This is a process by which individuals, organizations, countries, and so on organize in a way that allows economic and social goals to be met while also sustaining broader environmental goals. For instance, Accenture, a professional services company employing over 700,000 employees worldwide, is consistently ranked as one of the top ESG (environmental, social, and governance) companies.[13] It achieves this impressive ranking through innovative steps for embedding ESG into every aspect of value creation—from client and community relationships to internal business operations. One such innovation is the Accenture 360° Value Reporting Experience—"a holistic, integrated digital hub" involving "an unprecedented collaboration across [their] organization . . . including Finance, Investor Relations, Legal, Sustainability, Corporate

Citizenship, Human Resources, Global IT, Corporate Services & Sustainability, and Marketing."[14] The 360° reporting tool allows them to "measure value in all directions," share ESG progress, and maintain balance. Put simply, if sustainability is a tightrope, then sustainable development and ESG are the skills and equipment necessary to get on and stay on the rope.[15]

A good framework for establishing your sustainable development initiatives is the UN's 17 Sustainable Development Goals (SDGs). On January 1, 2016, the United Nations launched their 2030 Agenda for Sustainable Development, which includes 17 SDGs for addressing the three dimensions of sustainable development—economic, environmental, and social—as well as aspects related to effective institutions, justice, and peace.[16]

The SDGs are:

- No poverty;
- Zero hunger;
- Good health and well-being;
- Quality education;
- Gender equality;
- Clean water and sanitation;
- Affordable and clean energy;
- Decent work and economic growth;
- Industry, innovation, and infrastructure;
- Reduce inequalities;
- Sustainable cities and communities;
- Responsible consumption and production;
- Climate action;
- Life below water;
- Life on land;

- Peace, justice, and strong institutions; and

- Partnership for the goals.

As former UN Secretary-General Ban Ki-moon puts it, the goals are "our shared vision of humanity and a social contract between the world's leaders and the people"—namely, the 193 leaders who signed on to the agenda in September 2015. "They are a to-do list for people and planet, and a blueprint for success."[17]

SDGs help leaders prioritize actionable steps for achieving the best possible balance among all stakeholders. A complete business model using this blueprint for sustainable growth lays out a specific plan of action to maintain (long-term) performance. A sustainable model explicitly incorporates decision-making elements that emphasize social and ecological costs and benefits—in other words, it's a fundamental aspect of strategy, not a "bolt on."[18]

WHY SUSTAINABILITY IS IMPORTANT

Organizations are taking these bold steps because sustainability affects all aspects of performance. Outside of the obvious social and ecological importance, sustainability bolsters economic growth. EY research has found that companies that invest in a sustainable supply chain can boost their value chain revenue by 12–23%. Likewise, in its 2017 "Better Business, Better World" report, the Business and Sustainable Development Commission (BSDC) estimates that, if business leaders collectively achieve just four of the 17 UN SDGs—namely, sustainable food and agriculture, sustainable cities and urban mobility, clean and affordable energy and materials, and good health and well-being—they could unlock economic opportunities worth at least $12 trillion per year and up to 380 million new jobs (mostly in developing countries) by 2030.[19,20]

WHAT WE KNOW ABOUT SUSTAINABILITY

Fortunately, the international community has made progress toward this compelling future. According to the International Institute for Sustainable Development, G20 nations have committed at least

$368.18 billion to clean energy since early 2020. And, according to the Global Sustainable Investment Alliance, sustainable investing rose from $30.7 trillion in 2018 to $35.3 trillion in 2020—a 15% increase in just two years.[21,22]

In addition to large global investments in the SDGs, we know society at all levels is shifting priorities and behavior. Following are some examples of who cares and what they're doing to change.

Employees care about sustainability. The Internet is teeming with statistics espousing the positive impact of sustainability on key employee metrics. For example, a survey exploring employee performance in over 5,000 French firms found a 16–21% boost in productivity among workers at eco-friendly organizations. And an international survey of more than 14,000 people from nine countries found that 70% of employees are more likely to stay with an employer that prioritizes sustainability, and roughly half would accept a lower salary to work for these companies.[23,24]

Consumers care about sustainability. A large survey of over 10,000 consumers in 17 countries conducted by Simon-Kucher & Partners found that, between 2016 and 2021, 85% of consumers shifted their purchasing behavior to a more sustainable approach, such as actively searching for and choosing greener alternatives. In addition, 60% of consumers rated sustainability as a critical purchase factor—following price and quality.[25]

Leaders care about sustainability. Gartner finds sustainability is surging up the list of CEO priorities in the US—up from 13th (2020) to 8th (2022–2023).[26]

However, we also know there's a sizable gap between what leaders are saying and what they're doing. Putting numbers to this problem, an IBM survey of over 3,000 CEOs questioned worldwide found that 48% say sustainability is a top priority—though only 23% of respondents are broadly implementing sustainability strategies. And if that weren't enough, a recent Google-funded survey found that 58% of CEOs and other C-suite leaders around the world admitted their company was guilty of greenwashing—with the number rising to 68% among the US participants—even though they listed sustainability as a top priority.[27,28,29]

In brief, leaders have a long way to go before closing the gap between advocating sustainability and living sustainably.

One reason society has difficulties with this say-do gap is the tension between egoistic and altruistic tendencies. When egoistic tendencies are at play, interests for the greater good often fall by the wayside. And so, for us to achieve sustainability, our unparalleled talent for resource extraction needs to be matched with our equally impressive tendency for altruism if we are to close the divide. Culturally this plays out in several ways, such as in the tension among economic, ecological, and social bottom lines. For example, something's gotta give when it comes to the economic value of the beef industry—estimated at $136 billion just in the US—versus the sizable environmental costs of beef. Or something's gotta give when it comes to the economic value of the "fast fashion" industry—valued at over $90 billion worldwide—versus the social costs employees suffer (particularly women) in developing countries who are subjected to unacceptable labor and human rights violations.[30,31,32,33]

These tensions often lead to tactics to maintain unsustainable practices in the pursuit of profit, savings, convenience, and so on. Established tactics for resisting change include lobbying to minimize accountability (e.g., the beverage industry resisting a health-related tax on sugary drinks); creating political wedges between citizens to distract, divide, and delay progress (e.g., fossil fuel interests spreading disinformation to encourage climate denial and thus impede action); feigning sustainability with window dressing (e.g., the tobacco industry treating corporate social responsibility as mainly a public-relations exercise); and good old-fashioned fraud (e.g., the Volkswagen "Dieselgate" scandal, which has cost the company billions of dollars).[34]

Even well-intentioned individuals add to the problem. For example, many employees consume meals in disposable packaging and drive long solo commutes in vehicles designed for four or more. Consumers likewise contribute to unsustainable behavior with head-in-the-sand tactics, such as buying products from companies known to violate the human rights of workers in their supply chains. And then there are also the justifiable concerns of those on tight budgets who can't afford sustainable alternatives.[35,36,37,38]

The cold hard truth is that something's gotta give. The unsustainability of humanity's practices makes change unavoidable—either the soft way or the hard way. This is why a significant amount of multidisciplinary research is going into establishing systemic sustainability. For example, strategic management experts are developing frameworks for sustainable business models that outperform old-school models for creating short-term shareholder value. Organizational scientists are exploring new methods for increasing sustainable employee behavior, such as new ways of working in this post-pandemic world. And social psychologists are looking at why and how consumers "go green."[39,40,41]

This surge of research and broad public interest points in one direction: leaders need to coordinate the efforts of consumers, employees, and firms to avoid immediate and long-term pitfalls. An increasing body of evidence warns that critical tipping points related to climate change, economic volatility, and social unrest are fast approaching, and we must establish a steady transition strategy *now* if we're to avoid last-minute, rash decision-making. Otherwise, we'll experience a transition crunch—when a shock to the system abruptly triggers many crises at once. The pandemic, for instance, caught many organizations off guard, resulting in every possible weak link in their business being stressed to (near) failure. As such, leaders are now tasked with finding a balanced approach to decreasing unsustainable practices while increasing sustainable alternatives—an ambidexterity challenge known as the exploration-exploitation trade-off.[42,43,44,45]

This delicate trade-off is like threading a needle. Organizations can't move too quickly away from old certainties that give them a competitive advantage, but at the same time they can't rest on their laurels if they want to remain innovative and, ultimately, sustainable. A good example of lingering too long on an old certainty can be seen in how Nokia went from dominating the mobile phone market in 2007 (with a market share around 40%) to a measly 1% in 2015. It's widely thought that Nokia's downfall resulted from its top managers, who were complacent in their success, not comprehending what a game changer the iPhone was and favoring short-term profit over long-term development. Unfortunately, despite this case and *many* others like it, and despite the significant efforts of experts to warn of impending disruptions, too many corporations, industries, and even governments have yet to demonstrate how to balance ideal short-term results against sustainable long-term strategy.[46,47,48,49]

Given the rapidly increasing and overlapping nature of crises, it's essential that we learn how to effectively change our unsustainable course. To do that we must drill down into what we don't know in order to discover our deepest *unknown unknowns*.

WHAT WE DON'T KNOW ABOUT SUSTAINABILITY

Sadly, research on sustainable business models is disjointed. Scholars tend to focus on individual puzzle pieces rather than on what leaders really need: a clear understanding of how the pieces fit together to form systemic sustainability. For example, supply chain managers will be more inclined to switch from a just-in-time system to a "just-in-case" system if they can see the social, environmental, *and* economic value. As I'll discuss later, this is where intelligent management systems that map the entire supply chain in real time add value. They capture a bird's-eye view of operations so experts can find ways to simultaneously lower emissions, avoid bottlenecks, and reduce costs.[50]

The next hurdle to overcome is the lack of practical output regarding the value-add of sustainable business models. Though there is a growing body of work on the conceptual nature of what organizations can and *ought* to do, sufficient data is lacking regarding who's doing what and how it's working out in their organizations. Leaders do not have a road map on how to achieve systemic sustainability; they don't know how to find the place where economic, social, and environmental values converge. Simply put, the need to change is urgent, but we lack the tools necessary for change.

Fortunately, humanity has a powerful all-purpose solution when all else fails: leadership. Effective leadership drives change during times of complexity and uncertainty, and it can align individual and group interests. Surprisingly, however, little formal research has gone into how leadership can help business and society achieve their sustainable goals. Though there is a call for "broadening the theoretical basis of green [sustainability] leadership," we're missing a concrete understanding of how leadership drives sustainable change.[51,52]

There are many unanswered questions for researchers and practitioners to explore. For instance, what type of leadership is required when the realities of the next sustainability crunch take hold? Is distributed leadership necessary to oversee the complexity of sustainability? Or is a hierarchical structure better for the rapid pace of sustainability? Good, old-fashioned command and control might still have a place when decision-making speed is a factor. Also, how can organizations best handle simultaneous waves of transition? Many changes at once, even for the better, are jarring and disruptive.

What's needed is a practical road map for successfully implementing sustainability. Leaders need to find the shortest path to aligning individual and group interests. To follow, you'll find out how to quickly arrive at this destination using CLS.

CLS TECHNOLOGY AND SUSTAINABILITY

The writing is on the wall, and indeed something's gotta give. From severe political unrest to looming financial threats to ecological disasters, "business as *unusual*" is the new normal. It's a time of great uncertainty and complexity requiring a new type of leader who has both the courage to meet these challenges head-on and the vision to use any innovative solution necessary for success. This new type of leader is a CLS-driven leader who combines the latest in science and technology with valuable lessons learned from practice. Here are some examples of how you can become this visionary CLS-driven leader.

Challenge: Understanding the Ground Truth of Sustainability

Leaders can collect substantial amounts of active and passive data to gain better insights into employees', consumers', and society's wants and needs regarding sustainability. Active data includes comments individuals provide in employee pulse surveys, customer in-app surveys, and so on. It's a vast lake of data that leaders can leverage with natural language processing methods such as topic modeling and sentiment analysis. Using this computational approach, leaders find novel suggestions regarding sustainability that would otherwise remain hidden in a large jumble of data. You'll find patterns in ESG-related preferences and understand your stakeholders on a deeper level than what small focus groups and multiple-choice questions have to offer.[53]

CLS-driven leaders operating at this scale go far beyond focus groups and management by multiple choice. They find hidden gems of innovation by working with experts who are mining insights from vast amounts of active data. Scientists researching consumer electronics, for example, are uncovering clear consumer preferences in Amazon reviews for more sustainable next-gen goods with robust designs and easily replaceable parts in order to minimize e-waste. Other researchers are scanning large amounts of company reviews on platforms such as Glassdoor and Indeed for insights about living and working conditions that simultaneously promote employee well-being, productivity, and retention. Collectively what we're witnessing is a major shift in how leaders are using active data to make products, services, and business practices more engaging and sustainable.[54,55,56]

Passive data, on the other hand, is collected indirectly via browsing patterns, links shared, purchases, work behavior, and much more. This large quantity of data is often collected continuously in real time and offers up potentially surprising insights you wouldn't find using just active data. For example, my colleagues and I recently published a paper on sustainable behavior during COVID-19 using billions of aggregated and anonymized link shares and reshares on Facebook in the whole of the US over several months. We found that, though a majority of people in the US explicitly reported support for environmental sustainability on a large-scale survey (i.e., active data), those concerns took a back seat to COVID-19 when we passively analyzed what people were actually talking about on Facebook. Using passive data, you might find that consumers who explicitly espouse the value of sustainable products choose the less expensive, less sustainable option, or that employees who promote sustainability are reluctant to engage with green work initiatives because they're not sufficiently incentivized.[57,58]

This tendency to say one thing and do another when it comes to sustainability stems from a "social desirability bias"—people *want* to (appear to) be prosocial, but that doesn't change the fact that they also need to save money, time, and effort. Fortunately, if this say-do gap surfaces in the data, then leaders can use behavioral science—a core aspect of CLS—to bridge the divide. You can accomplish this mission with brand ambassadors to socially influence sustainability. You can also use timely prompts and incentives to promote sustainable behavior or work to increase "green knowledge" among your stakeholders so they better understand the consequences of their actions.[59,60]

Challenge: Monitoring, Improving, and Maintaining Sustainable Operations

CLS also enables leaders to collect substantial amounts of data to pinpoint systemic threats to organizational sustainability. For example, you can continuously track daily carbon emissions at every point in a supply chain via "process mining," which combines data science and process management so as to discover, monitor, and improve processes. You can use these AI-powered platforms to sleuth out opportunities to improve performance—such as finding suppliers with more eco-friendly production practices or introducing automated processes that continually work on optimizing logistics.[61]

Process mining will ultimately help you achieve systemic sustainability. You can see how well your organization is keeping supply chains moving in times of crisis, removing human rights violations in the supply chain, maintaining employee and customer engagement, and incorporating innovative carbon-reducing technology. It's one thing to lead a company based on independent parts of your business model (i.e., evaluating puzzle pieces); it's a game-changing shift to lead a company based on a clear set of systemic practices (i.e., evaluating how well your organization's puzzle pieces fit together).

This bird's-eye view allows for precise adjustments to operations— which is exceedingly important because sustainable business models will not spontaneously emerge. They require innovations to gather, synthesize, analyze, and act upon organization-wide data. By taking this CLS step, you will gain next-level vision and help usher in a much more sustainable future.

Challenge: Accurately and Precisely Modeling Sustainable Transitions in a Low-Risk, High-Payoff Environment

Digital twins are another exciting advancement for getting at systemic sustainability. These "mirror worlds" combine vast amounts of real-time, historical, and simulated data to create a space where leaders can explore various paths to new business models. Porsche, for example, used this technology to digitally twin their materials with the goal of "mimicking the physical supply chain and reflecting the manufacturing processes along the lifecycle of the product." By twinning their supply chain, they can safely experiment with and work to improve sustainability in a simulated environment. This technology will revolutionize the ability to map the dynamics of systemic sustainability, such as how a leader's decisions can ripple out and affect factors such as manufacturing costs, carbon emissions, and consumer sentiment. It's a low-risk way to stress-test and optimize your ESG strategy.[62,63,64]

What's learned through these simulations you can then use to establish deeper and richer dialogue with your stakeholders. You can build your mirror world with consumers and employees, for instance, so they understand firsthand how critical factors change over time, what trade-offs emerge, and how various decisions affect important variables such as product price, quality, availability, and sustainability. They go on a journey with you in a game-like environment to co-create sustainable outcomes. This will skyrocket stakeholder engagement and confirm your status as an ultramodern leader.

As a way of easing into this CLS-driven world of sustainability, let's now turn our attention to how one of the most innovative chocolate manufacturers in the world is leading the way in sustainable business practices.

SUSTAINABILITY Q&A WITH TONY'S CHOCOLONELY

"We want to completely push out anonymity from the cocoa supply chain so unsustainable practices have nowhere to hide. We want to create full transparency from bean to bar."
—Paul Schoenmakers, Head of Impact, Tony's Chocolonely

Sustainability is one of those issues connecting all people, businesses, and societies. Humanity is unavoidably interconnected in everything from huge world events to the everyday pleasures we take for granted. Something as simple as enjoying a piece of chocolate, for example, has far-reaching global implications regarding sustainability, and leaders must understand this delicate balance of costs and benefits if they want to survive and thrive into the future.

To capture this intricate web of connectivity—even in the seemingly simple pleasures of modern society—I had the exciting opportunity to speak with Paul Schoenmakers, Head of Impact for Tony's Chocolonely—the largest chocolate brand in the Netherlands.

Some readers may not have heard of Tony's Chocolonely yet, though the company is expanding. But you will likely know some of the partners it has recruited to make chocolate 100% modern-slavery free. Using Tony's "Open Chain" way-of-working, companies such as the global discount supermarket chain Aldi and the much-loved ice cream company Ben & Jerry's have aligned with Tony's five sourcing principles, which I'll touch on shortly. Their products are also available at well-known retailers such as Target in the US and Tesco in the UK. Tony's continued efforts for excellence in sustainability, such as its Open Chain approach, has also resulted in numerous awards. In 2022, for instance, the company was rated as best in class on the global "Chocolate Scorecard," a ranking of the world's biggest chocolate companies. It even has a shoe and apparel line in partnership with Adidas to promote an end to modern slavery in the chocolate industry.

To sum it up, Tony's may not be as big as some of the other companies showcased in the other chapters, but pound-for-pound it is an innovative powerhouse when it comes to sustainability. Now, let's take a look at what sets it apart.

Q: What sustainability challenge or opportunity is of most interest to your organization?

A: Tony's is committed to changing the norm in the cocoa industry. For example, we want to end extreme poverty among farmers, illegal labor, forced labor, and deforestation.

Q: What specific question(s) do you have regarding your organization's ability to address sustainability?

A: How can we help break the poverty cycle from one generation to the next? How can we increase awareness? How can we lead by example? How can we source cocoa in a mutually beneficial way using Tony's five sourcing principles?

The five principles are:

1. Ensuring cocoa beans are traceable;
2. Paying a higher price (a living-income price);
3. Building stronger farmer cooperatives;
4. Creating long-term business relationships with farmers; and
5. Improving productivity and quality by supporting the professionalization of farmers.

Finally, how can we inspire to act? Specifically, how best can we share our entire supply chain operations and knowledge base with competitors so they are more likely to join our way of working—that is, Tony's Open Chain initiative.

Q: What specific expectations do you have about what's influencing your organization's ability to address sustainability?

A: Our focus on mission first, profit second is driving our ability to address sustainability. We don't want to maximize profit at the expense of human rights. Consumers see this commitment and it's made us a leader in the Netherlands, and now we're growing quickly in the UK, the US, and German-speaking regions.

Q: What data and tech are you using to address sustainability?

A: We started our traceable supply chain in 2012. At that time, many industry leaders said it was not possible to create such a level of traceability because of the many cocoa sources. However, working with the IT company ChainPoint, we developed "Beantracker." It's a transparent platform where all players present in the network see and enter information to trace every step from "bean to bar." It's about 100% traceability, and anyone we work with in our supply chain has to participate in Beantracker. Also, in 2015, we started mapping out our most important indicators and defined 15 non-financial KPIs in 2015 (of which traceability is number one).

Partnering with the Impact Institute and True Price, we also calculate our carbon footprint from bean to bar. Then, working with JustDigIt, a nonprofit working to regreen Africa, we invest in their initiative to offset our full carbon footprint. Now, we are also more focused on reducing our carbon footprint entirely.

We're also working with all cooperatives so they can GPS-map their members' lands, estimate yield, and mitigate deforestation by avoiding encroachment. We can then combine this data with satellite images to look at changes in the canopy and introduce shade trees where necessary to capture more carbon. This is all part of our efforts to reduce the carbon footprint of chocolate.

Q: What drove your data and tech choices (e.g., personal decision, team decision, data scientist decision, using what's available, some sort of systematic process for selecting data and tech)?

A: It's partly when we feel like we need to do something to improve things. Also, we are constantly looking for gaps in sustainable performance and experimenting to find solutions. In 2013, for example, we discovered that "just paying the Fairtrade Premium" wasn't getting farmers out of poverty. We then challenged ourselves to pay even more to farmers. We started with doubling the premium. We also formalized this initiative by developing a model to measure cost of living to refine the process. The outcome was Tony's "living income model for cocoa." Premiums have increased further and we now pay more than 60% on top of the conventional cocoa price to close the living income gap.

Q: What sort of data and/or tech are you using to track the impact of your sustainability initiatives over time?

A: Everything I mentioned previously, such as Tony's Open Chain and the living income model. All of these innovations have a temporal component. Every year we also publish our nonfinancial KPIs—which are independently assured by PwC—for us and others to monitor change over time.

Q. What sort of data and/or tech are you using to track your sustainability initiatives at multiple levels?

A: Twice a year we conduct an elaborate employee survey with help from our partner Effectory to understand how our mission affects our employees' motivation, engagement, and commitment at all levels. We find that staying focused on our mission is a major source of employee well-being. We also monitor how our customers feel about our performance, and we work to spread our traceable-open-chain approach to other companies such as sellers.

Q: What sort of data and/or tech are you using to track DEI aspects of your sustainability initiatives?

A: We publish "Tony's Chocolonely Annual FAIR Report," which details every aspect of our DEI efforts—from cocoa farmer relationships to internal company practices.

Q: What is the (expected) outcome of your tech-enabled plans for sustainability?

A: We are focused on data ownership. The farmers data should be owned by the farmers and their cooperatives. For example, we make sure they have complete ownership of GPS data, traceability data, and child-labor-monitoring data so they can use it to steer their organizations. That's quite different from how other companies do it because they also see that data as a new profit generator.

They are getting this huge amount of data and keeping it for themselves. Instead, it's all about farmer agency and building their capacity to collect, use, and share the data. The cooperative is in a central role, and we work in partnership with them. Short story, the source of the data owns the data. Finally, we want to completely push out anonymity from the cocoa supply chain so unsustainable practices have nowhere to hide. We want to create full transparency from bean to bar.

Concluding Thoughts about My Interview with Paul Schoenmakers

Tony's mission to disrupt the sustainability status quo drives its innovative use of data and its development of tech. The company wants to break the (chocolate) mold, and it's reflected in their pursuit of new digital tools such as their Beantracker and Open Chain technologies. From the start, it remained mission-focused on transparency when others said change isn't possible. Instead, as is often the case, innovation prevailed. CLS-driven leaders need this level of courage, determination, and digital resourcefulness to create a sustainable future. I therefore strongly encourage you to develop these traits so you can take your place in the pantheon of great visionary (and sustainable) leaders.

CHAPTER 5

Leading Through Crisis, Crisis, and More Crisis

Every morning when I turn on the news it seems there's another global event subverting any semblance of stability. Liz Truss's profoundly flawed economic plan ended in the shortest Prime Minister tenure in British history (six weeks!). Small businesses everywhere are struggling to return to pre-pandemic form. And there's so much to say about the catastrophic environmental, social, and economic effects of climate change. I could write an entire book about the human face of crisis, but that won't help us find opportunities in the darkness. Leaders need to look past the gloom of perpetual crisis and find solutions to the overlapping challenges testing us like never before.

This is a defining moment for leaders. Organizations are increasingly confronted with tidal waves of disruption affecting everything from global supply chains to individual well-being. Crises such as the violence of the 2022 war in Ukraine quickly spread via interconnected economic, ecological, and social pathways to trigger additional dangers such as unsustainable energy prices in Europe, humanitarian concerns in refugee camps, and a global food crisis. The outcome is a world filled with events we can no longer avoid or ignore. Everything will affect you and your organization—whether you know about it or not. That's why it's so important to become a digitally-minded leader. To successfully anticipate, address, mitigate, and even benefit from the biggest and most complex challenges of our time, we need to lead with advancements in science and tech. Computational leadership science (CLS) provides you with the necessary lens to see the full scope of a particular crisis and its impact on your organization.[1]

Ensuring you have this CLS-enabled vision is critical for sustainable growth in troublesome times. According to the World Economic Forum's Global Risk Perception Survey 2022, most risk experts and world leaders in business, government, and civil society are worried (23%) or at least concerned (61%) with the "outlook for the world." And, overall, 89% of the respondents have a negative "outlook for the world over the next three years." Similarly, more than 70% of businesses who participated in PwC's 2021 Global Crisis Survey reported experiencing negative impacts stemming from the pandemic and that they plan to increase investment in resilience. In other words, almost every expert in the world is worried about crisis, and most leaders are investing in new ways to deal with (and even benefit from) these inevitable events.[2]

This upheaval represents an opportunity for you to become a next-level leader. It's a "challenging job demand" (see the Chapter 3, "Breaking the Death-by-Meeting Curse and Other Engagement Killers") that's going to help you grow personally and professionally. To help you with this growth, I'll first explain what we know—and don't know—about crisis. Then I'll provide some examples of how you can utilize CLS-driven data and tech to extract benefit where others see cost. I'll conclude with a Q&A session I had with the Director of Enterprise Resilience and Crisis Management at Microsoft.

WHAT WE KNOW ABOUT CRISIS

Crisis can be defined as a "serious threat to the basic structures or the fundamental values and norms of a system, which under time pressure and highly uncertain circumstances necessitates making vital decisions."[3] Note also that a crisis can emerge from an actual event or even just the perception of a threat. Perceived threat driven by misinformation, for example, can radicalize individuals and lead to terrorist attacks. A particular crisis is also defined by its cause, location, size, and duration, as well as the response. Some crises are relatively brief and manageable, while others are catastrophic and unresolvable. Many are also unexpected and highly disruptive. The true test is understanding how to lead through a varied landscape of disruption.[4,5,6]

Framing Crisis with Existing Models

The first step is developing an effective model for managing crisis. Crisis expert Professor W. Timothy Coombs, for example, defines *crisis management* as "a set of factors designed to combat crises and to lessen the actual damage inflicted by a crisis."[7] It's commonly broken down into three phases—pre-crisis, in-crisis, and post-crisis—which involve four interrelated factors: prevention, preparation, response, and revision.[8] This overlaps with *crisis leadership*—which is the process of activating leaders and followers and coordinating their behavior for the best possible outcome. For example, both leaders and followers will emerge to address a financial crisis, and they will have to organize their interactions in a way that allows them to deal with and grow from the event.[9]

To frame this dynamic, my group at Harvard's National Preparedness Leadership Initiative (NPLI) developed the concept "meta-leadership." This involves a multidimensional process of leading through crisis by leading up to superiors, leading across to peers, leading down to subordinates, and leading beyond to external stakeholders. It's a holistic framework for mapping the complexities of crisis leadership and identifying specific areas in need of improvement. For instance, meta-leadership works to remove the power barriers between top leadership and frontline managers to drastically increase the speed at which real-time information gets up to superiors.[10]

Given this need to operate across multiple channels, I define effective *crisis leaders* as those who are able to lead in any direction necessary so as to coordinate and influence others toward a mutually beneficial outcome. These leaders are able to address the phases of crisis using an adaptive toolbox of leadership traits and styles—from empathy and charisma to command-and-control authority—depending on the situation and the audience. They're also willing and able to deploy the CLS-inspired tools and techniques I touch on later. In short, a successful crisis response requires a highly effective crisis leader.

The Realities of Crisis

Though practitioners and researchers put much effort into framing crisis and understanding how to lead through it, the hard truth is that business and society are unprepared for what's to come. For instance, in PwC's 2020 Annual Corporate Directors Survey, which gauged the views of almost 700 US directors in September of that year, only 37% of the respondents said their board had a strong understanding of their organizations' crisis management plan. Similarly, a 2022 Edelman survey of over 300 chief marketing officers and chief communication officers from around the globe found that 60% reported not having the necessary skill sets in their staff to address the many types of crises they're facing today. Essentially, the pandemic and the economic fallout were stress tests, and this data clearly indicates that leadership processes are not prepared.[11,12]

There's no other way to say it: this is bad, for so many reasons. Here are just a few mind-blowing facts and figures emphasizing the critical need for crisis preparedness:

- In 2022, Swiss Re, the world's largest reinsurer, reported a total global economic loss of $270 billion and insured losses of $111 billion due to natural disasters in 2021. It also notes this "continues the long-term trend of insured losses increasing by an average of 5–7% annually worldwide."[13]

- According to Cybersecurity Ventures, costs related to cyber-crime—a crisis of malevolence—is estimated to reach as high as $10.5 trillion by 2025. That's more than the combined GDP of every country except the US and China.[14]

- Crisis can have long-lasting effects. Chernobyl—one of the most expensive disasters in human history—already has an estimated cost of over $700 billion, and the costs will continue to mount for several thousands of years due to ongoing maintenance of the plant and the surrounding land. Furthermore, the World Health Organization points out that, as of June 2022, Chernobyl is currently in an active war zone—along with 17 other nuclear reactors, radioactive waste facilities, and radio-nuclear hazards.[15]

Speaking of Ukraine and the interdependent nature of crises, the International Monetary Fund expects the current war and associated humanitarian crisis in Ukraine will slow global recovery from the pandemic crisis—leading to a significant reduction in annual growth, continued inflation, and worsening of problems such as the affordable housing crisis. The compounding effects of crises illuminates the "transboundary" challenge leaders face when dealing with critical events. These crises are not just humanitarian, not just public health, not just socioeconomic—they form wicked synergies generating combined effects greater than the sum of their respective parts.[16,17]

Fortunately, the last word is a positive one. Though crisis is costly, it's also a vital opportunity to change and grow. Crisis motivates experts to dig deeper into the complexity of a situation in order to find new solutions, and crisis sets the stage for game-changing data and tech to turbocharge leadership.

The Science of Crisis

Crisis research is rapidly expanding due to unprecedented global events such as war, pandemics, and climate change. Emerging topics of interest include "community resilience"—a group's ability to thrive in crisis situations by knowing how to adapt effectively—and "creeping crisis"—understanding how, when, and why a simmering crisis underneath the surface suddenly explodes.[18,19,20]

COVID-19 is a great example of how a creeping crisis and the lack of community resilience can converge to create a sudden explosion of disruption. As the former head of the US Strategic National Stockpile, Greg Burel, put it in 2020, "Right now, [the medical] market runs on a just-in-time basis, because it is optimized for the best possible cost. . . . But sometimes getting the best possible cost leaves you in a position that you have the worst possible preparedness." This example highlights how leadership favored economic factors, which diminished resilience and put society on a path to abrupt, catastrophic failure once the pandemic hit.[21,22]

Another area gaining more attention since the pandemic is "transboundary crisis management," wherein interconnected challenges require interconnected, de-siloed solutions. Sticking with the pandemic example, de-siloed solutions involve the obvious players such as virologists and epidemiologists being joined by social psychologists, organizational scientists, economists, and other social scientists to break down barriers such as vaccine hesitancy and health care systems prioritizing profits over preparedness.[23]

It's this ability to envision and orchestrate de-siloed, adaptive problem-solving that unequivocally separates great crisis leaders from the crowd. As I'll discuss in the section on applying CLS, you can use data and tech both to boost your situational awareness and to coordinate a next-level crisis response. You'll be able to see a creeping crisis coming from a mile away, you'll create and execute a superior transboundary plan, and you'll solidify your reputation as the go-to person for preparedness and resilience.

Stakeholder Engagement and Learning from Crisis

Indeed, establishing yourself as a great crisis leader increases your reputation (and the reputation of your organization). But note: this is not a vanity issue. Building and maintaining a good reputation during times of crisis has an impact on how stakeholders react—employees stay engaged, customers remain loyal, value increases, and overall resilience improves. Such outcomes are the result of purposeful and authentic leadership practices.[24] As my father drilled into my head: "Don't talk about it, be about it!"

One aspect of "being about it" in terms of crisis preparedness and response is corporate social responsibility (CSR). Understanding the priorities and challenges of diverse stakeholders helps you create a balanced response. In a study on leading through COVID-19, my colleagues from Harvard's NPLI and I found a consistent pattern: effective leaders across various sectors and industries—from aviation and energy to education and retail—continuously connect with diverse stakeholders up, down, across, and beyond the organization using the meta-leadership framework mentioned earlier. They always consider the views of their stakeholders, which enables them to gain and maintain accurate situational insights from various perspectives.[25,26]

Great crisis leaders take this multidimensional perspective and engage in "double-loop learning"—learning that involves fundamentally changing underlying assumptions and mindsets to make the organization better prepared for the next crisis. Here are just two examples of their lasting mindset shifts stemming from the pandemic. In a single-loop mindset, managers—not necessarily leaders—refine existing practices such as how to optimize the performance of physically present employees or how to further tweak lean supply chains. They want to maintain business as usual. But a leader with a double-loop mindset appreciates how physical presence in the workplace doesn't necessarily equate to performance and how, in times of perpetual disruption, cost-oriented just-in-time supply chains must give way to investment-oriented "just-in-case" alternatives. These leaders have their eye on the new normal and meet it head-on.[27,28,29]

Crisis leaders also rise to the challenges at each phase of an event. In the pre-crisis phase, they minimize the chance of crisis through early detection, and they prepare for events by clearly communicating what everyone's unique roles will be when inevitable shocks do occur. In the crisis phase, they effectively lead their people through adversity with adaptive processes that incorporate information and modify plans of action in real time. And in the post-crisis phase they engage in double-loop learning in order to capitalize on unexpected silver linings to make lasting change—such as the pandemic-induced push to remote working, which has created many opportunities for innovative leaders.

WHAT WE DON'T KNOW ABOUT CRISIS

Unfortunately, there are several blind spots making innovative crisis leadership the exception rather than the norm:

> EXPERTS HAVE A LIMITED UNDERSTANDING OF WHAT IT TAKES TO EFFECTIVELY TRANSITION FROM ONE PHASE OF A CRISIS TO THE NEXT. Practitioners and researchers tend to focus on particular phases of crisis in isolation rather than understanding it as a continuous process across the three phases of pre-crisis, in-crisis, and post-crisis. This "process blind spot" can restrict your understanding of how to successfully navigate the phases of crisis. For example, research demonstrates the value of char-ismatic leadership during the emergence and peak of crisis with a steady decline as the event transitions to the post-crisis

phase. However, little is known about exactly when the charismatic rhetoric should ramp up and when it's time for crisis leaders to place more emphasis on using directive authority to create stability, structure, and order.[30,31,32]

EXPERTS DON'T FULLY UNDERSTAND HOW DIVERSE STAKEHOLDERS REACT TO CRISIS. Factors such as cultural background, socioeconomic status, and proximity to the threat will influence how stakeholders perceive and respond to the same crisis—so you will benefit from tailoring your crisis leadership to meet their needs. The regional and political differences regarding COVID-19 beliefs in the US are prime examples of how diverging backgrounds influence the perception of crisis—and how leaders need to personalize their approach to guide a diverse audience.[33]

EXPERTS TEND TO FOCUS ON INDIVIDUAL EVENTS RATHER THAN THE CONNECTIONS BETWEEN CRISES. This narrow approach to understating crisis reduces generalizability and cumulative learning from previous events. Crisis leaders lack an effective framework for identifying hidden connections between crises, which subsequently increases the chance of reinventing the crisis-response wheel from one event to the next.

This blind spot is especially relevant in times of large-scale, interconnected crises when seemingly unrelated events can disrupt local operations in your organization, such as how the war in Ukraine, climate change, and COVID-19 collectively increase employee stress and ultimately turnover. For example, a "Stress in America" survey conducted by the American Psychological Association in February 2022 found that 73% of respondents "are overwhelmed by the number of crises" and 71% "have gotten better at prioritizing what is important to them." In other words, people are stressed and work engagement has bottomed out, in part, because leaders lack a playbook for helping employees cope with compounding threats.[34,35]

EXPERTS REQUIRE NEW METHODS FOR CAPTURING THE COMPLEXITY OF CRISIS LEADERSHIP. Little is known about the dynamics of "transboundary collaboration," which cuts across geographic, policy, political, cultural, language, and legal borders. The necessary tools for mapping and navigating complex crises, as well as the platforms necessary for effective de-siloed communication, just aren't available. Further, many of the frameworks for understanding crisis and leading through it have not changed much for over 70 years. As a result, we have an outdated crisis-management system that does a poor job of (a) accumulating knowledge about complex and overlapping crises and (b) translating that knowledge into high-impact solutions. In other words, you're expected to build modern homes with stone-aged tools. This is in no way a critique of your performance; you're likely doing an amazing job—which is why you were chosen for the job. I just want to demonstrate the need for updated systems to remove unnecessary barriers.[36,37,38,39]

Great leaders are compelled to seek out and remove these blind spots because they know the value of going past the reactive façade of crisis management. For example, you can address the war in Ukraine (even if your organization is far removed) by providing employees with opportunities to process their anxiety via fundraisers, awareness campaigns, and other forms of giving. The outcomes of such efforts, as noted by the Cleveland Clinic, can include decreased depression and stress—which are the precursors of turnover—as well as increased self-esteem, happiness, and satisfaction—which are the drivers of sustainable performance. In short, you can take a war you seemingly have no control over and use it as an opportunity to boost social awareness and employee self-esteem. Taking such measures displays your concern for employee well-being and communicates your status as a next-level crisis leader.[40]

CLS AND NEXT-LEVEL CRISIS LEADERSHIP

To help you usher in this new era of crisis leadership, let's have a look at how CLS can boost performance across the three phases of crisis: pre-crisis, in-crisis, and post-crisis.

Challenge: Pre-crisis Leadership

In the pre-crisis phase, it's important to detect various types of creeping crises early so as to identify unsustainable practices and prevent (or at least mitigate) catastrophe. Fortunately, the use of data and tech amplifies a leader's ability to stay out in front. Here are some examples:

DETECTING CLIMATE CRISIS: The EU's Global Flood Awareness System (GloFAS), for example, aids in flood-threat detection by combining large amounts of meteorological data with hydrological models. This data and computational process is very important for spotting in advance the increasing number of floods throughout the world so that proactive steps can be taken. Such systems can provide leaders with ongoing, detailed, localized data to better anticipate the threat of flooding throughout their supply chain. Leaders using these increasingly accurate systems can then rapidly prepare stakeholders in hotspots and swiftly adjust operations as threats emerge from one location to the next. Relatedly, scientists are transforming complex climate projection data into impact models for sectors such as agriculture, forestry, and water. These advanced impact models will help leaders *avoid* risk, help them allocate resources to *prepare* for the effects of climate change, and help them continuously *optimize* decisions in complex, fast-changing environments.[41,42]

DETECTING FINANCIAL CRISIS: Big data and advancements in computational science are also increasing society's ability to detect early warning signals of financial crises and take early action to stem the tide of economic chaos. Harvard Business School's Behavioral Finance & Financial Stability Project, for example, has data on financial crises for more than 70 countries back to 1800 for researchers and practitioners wanting to explore complex patterns over time and place. Scientists are also using techniques such as machine learning and network analysis to analyze (global) financial behavior and interdependencies—that is, how the financial actions of one country or organization affect others—to predict crisis. Leaders can use this emerging research to identify and put a stop to risky behavior, improve portfolio selection, and prepare sooner for inevitable shocks. Leveraging big data with advanced data analytics is an opportunity for CLS-driven leaders to create unmatched financial performance and resilience.[43,44]

DETECTING ESG CRISIS: Leaders can incorporate tech such as the Internet of Things (IoT) and process mining—a data-driven technique for mapping operations—to continuously monitor and improve environmental, social, and governance (ESG) factors in their business. A good example of this is the Beantracker system of Tony's Chocolonely (discussed in the previous chapter on sustainability). The chocolate company uses the system to track its entire operations from bean to bar. This allows it to quickly detect any threats to its best-in-class ESG value chain and take immediate action to ensure the human rights, the working conditions, and the premium pay of the farmers it works with. Leaders using IoT and process mining to map their organization can, for example, automatically track water usage in their organization, proactively conduct cybersecurity stress testing throughout their operations, and rapidly assess whether their business processes comply with laws and regulations.[45,46,47.48,49,50]

DETECTING HUMANITARIAN CRISIS: The International Crisis Group offers "CrisisWatch"—a real-time global tracker of conflict-related crisis to aid in identifying trends, risks, and opportunities. Let's say you have suppliers in potential conflict regions. The escalation of tension could grind your operations to a halt, especially if the region provides mission-critical components, so it's important you have excellent situational awareness. This kind of "anytime, anywhere" analysis of disruptive events, such as the effect of conflict on your supply chain, could be an important tool in your toolbox. It could mean the difference between making sluggish and detrimental decisions versus making agile and proactive adjustments to operations. Also, in keeping with ESG values, CrisisWatch will help you surgically promote peace as tensions shift around the world.[51]

This vast pool of crisis data combined with modern analytics has great potential for fundamentally changing and improving pre-crisis leadership. This confluence will allow you to make better decisions when it comes to avoiding risk, preparing for shocks, and finding opportunities where others might see problems. You'll also have a better understanding of the dynamics at play leading up to a crisis—for example, the triggers escalating a creeping crisis—and how pulling a lever at your disposal will boost community resilience, such as promoting peace in conflict regions to safeguard your people and supply chains.

This CLS-driven approach can help you better predict the emergence of crisis and its ripple effects and help you optimize your pre-crisis leadership. Bottom line: if one aspect of a great crisis leader is vision, then you need to adopt these emerging techniques to maintain your vantage point in front of an increasingly chaotic world.

Challenge: In-crisis Leadership

Unfortunately, crisis is going to happen. All the pre-crisis prepping in the world, though necessary, isn't going to prevent bad things from happening. So, it's really a matter of how adaptive and responsive your team is once you're in a crisis. Here are some examples of how CLS increases your ability to swiftly adjust decision making when the proverbial hits the fan.

> COVID-19 RESPONSES: During the height of the pandemic, the Johns Hopkins COVID-19 Dashboard was a valuable source of information for gaining a real-time understanding of regional hotspots around the globe. Leaders frequently relied on this resource to assess trends, to cut through the noise of misinformation, and to make responsible decisions regarding employees and operations. Another helpful dashboard is the COVID-19 Global Gender Response Tracker. This tracker focuses on women's participation in COVID-19 task forces and regional policy measures for ensuring the safety and security of women. For example, business leaders using this tracker in the US could monitor what particular states were doing (or not doing) to support women during the lockdown and work

to supplement any regional deficits for their employees, such as providing a list of services for victims of domestic violence. Such innovations are important tools for the next major public-health crisis.[52,53,54]

NETWORKED RESPONSES: Gathering the necessary data for superior crisis response requires a systemic approach. That means always connecting with those below, above, across, and externally beyond so that you can increase and implement effective crisis leadership. For example, my colleagues and I are working with the alumni of Harvard's NPLI (again, the National Preparedness Leadership Initiative) to create the NPLI NetworkMap. The tool is a digital platform with clear visualizations to rapidly find experts in times of need. An NPLI alum dealing with a complex crisis can input any number of keywords and the NetworkMap will instantly identify those in the network who specialize in the keywords of interest. The user can then send individual messages or group messages to engage their fellow alum. Like white blood cells fighting infections, the platform helps you quickly wrap expertise around crisis.

GRANULAR AND TAILORED RESPONSES: As I've mentioned throughout this chapter, it's important to contingently switch between various leader traits, behaviors, and styles across the crisis life cycle. The challenge, however, is understanding where and when to switch. One solution is to use automated sentiment analysis of communication streams—for example, the level of positivity or negativity on social media, on employee slack channels, and on customer reviews—in order to detect patterns in such data and rapidly adjust your leadership accordingly.

As an example, the majority of rail traffic in the Netherlands—a primary means of transportation in the country—failed on May 31, 2021, stranding thousands of people everywhere in the country on their way home from school and work. A Dutch start-up using sentiment analysis was able to detect live customer reactions of this public unrest on social media, which revealed an initial reaction of frustration among those in urban areas and fear among those in rural areas with limited transportation options.[55,56]

The railway provider could've used this real-time information to automatically send tailored messages; for example, urban customers would've benefitted from having their frustration acknowledged while rural customers would've benefited from messages alleviating their fear of not getting home. The outcome of this approach would've been a much more reassuring, helpful, and personal response to the crisis. Using data and tech to gain this sort of advantage is what CLS is all about. You engage deeply with your stakeholders at scale and provide them with an extraordinary level of support.

The key takeaway regarding CLS during the in-crisis phase is that data and tech can boost your ability to make global yet granular responses that stream in information and knowledge from a vast network of people—all of which offers you an impressive leap forward in leading through crisis.

Challenge: Post-crisis Leadership

The many crises humanity has faced represents an amazing learning opportunity, and these challenges have pushed leaders to innovate new solutions. Here are some examples of learning new ways to deal with post-crisis stress—and then learning to shift mindsets so you're prepared for whatever comes next.

LEARNING TO MANAGE STRESS: Effective employee stress management is an important concern that emerges during crisis and carries over into the post-crisis phase. Unfortunately, most of the popular emerging technology for addressing employee well-being is potentially creepy or even invasive, such as employer-monitored apps that attempt to track their employees' every emotion throughout the day, as well as tech that measures stress by keeping track of employees' electrodermal activity, heart rate, and temperature. Though these approaches might seem to be helpful, the fact that this technology employs excessive monitoring might ironically contribute to stress rather than reduce it.

An alternative is using tech to promote positive steps for improving well-being. The Cleveland Clinic encourages the practice of "selling yourself to yourself." As they put it, "Remind yourself of what you do well." As a CLS-driven crisis leader, you can promote this healthy sense of self-esteem—and ultimately well-being—using chatbots or other minimally invasive prompts to occasionally ask employees for a few positive words about their efforts at home or work. The bot, for example, can ask an employee to list three things they're proud of accomplishing at work today. Note, however, those positive words are just for them—leave employee sentiment analysis and topic modeling out of this one.[57]

LEARNING TO LEARN: AI-supported triple-loop learning is a CLS process for completely redefining what is known. As mentioned earlier, leaders using a single-loop approach to post-pandemic learning are thinking about how to get the best out of people when they come back to the office. That is, they're using their pre-pandemic mindset. Double-loop leaders are thinking about how to transform mindsets and get the best out of people in a hybrid situation. Now, going further, triple-loop leaders are fundamentally questioning the relationship between work— be it physical, hybrid, or fully remote—and performance. As Korn Ferry puts, given the "augmenting of humans with machines . . . the focus now is less on the jobs employees perform and more on the capabilities people and technology can offer." In other words, performance has less to do with where employees work and more to do with how humans co-create with AI. For example, how employees interact with ChatGPT and other generative AI to develop new and innovative products and services is redefining what it means to be a high performer. It's truly a next-level mindset, and it will become the norm for how leaders judge and drive performance.[58,59]

Here's an example: Nasdaq launched a human-AI surveillance system to avoid crises related to trading activities and manipulative behavior. This collaboration is important because working alone, the AI side might find impractically complex or unrealistic pathways for solving problems, while the solo analyst might overlook new patterns of risky or fraudulent actions. But working together, they can collectively create a better framework for identifying crisis and developing workable solutions for mitigating future events. The AI synthesizes the patterns it finds in large, complex data with the human feedback it receives in order to learn new models for detecting threats. Analysts, on the other hand, have the opportunity to adjust—or entirely change—their understanding of ever-evolving financial crimes based on the AI's output and their capacity to create realistic solutions. This human-AI future will revolutionize how we learn from crisis, the pace at which we learn, and the scale of knowledge we can retain for future events.[60]

LEARNING TO PREPARE: Finally, humans and machines working together will skyrocket collective intelligence for future events. AI makes this possible by serving as a constantly updating repository of large-scale knowledge. Leaders can rely on this smart archive to both detect the signals of a creeping crisis and identify previously successful responses to similar events. For example, an intelligent system could compare real-time public health data with known patterns of how COVID-19 emerged and spread to detect faint signals of a pandemic. Humans and AI can then work together to simulate interventions and respond to threats with exceptional accuracy by improving estimations and projections for factors such as infectious disease dynamics, employee health outcomes, and impact on operations. This human-machine collaboration is pre-crisis preparedness at its finest.[61,62,63]

I'm extremely excited about where this collaborative future is going. Organizations are taking major steps to innovate next-gen solutions to deal with a world in perpetual crisis. As an example, let's turn our attention to Microsoft and see what it's doing to thrive in turbulent times.

CRISIS LEADERSHIP Q&A WITH MICROSOFT

"Intuition is always part of things, but data and tech drives clarity and alignment in the fog of crisis."
—*Jennie Clinton, Director of Enterprise Resilience and Crisis Management at Microsoft*

Crisis leadership has come to the forefront in many organizations since the COVID-19 pandemic. To discuss this invaluable process of leading through crisis I was fortunate to speak with Jennie Clinton, Director of Enterprise Resilience and Crisis Management at Microsoft.

Microsoft Corporation employs over 220,000 people worldwide and operates in 190 (out of 195) countries. Thus, given the immense size and geographic sprawl of the company, it's constantly tracking and addressing crisis—from small-scale issues with a single supplier to interconnected, global threats posed by pandemics and wars. As Microsoft states on its website regarding COVID-19, "We are working to do our part by ensuring the safety of our employees, striving to protect the health and well-being of the communities in which we operate, and providing technology and resources to our customers to help them do their best work." In other words, Microsoft's commitment to overcoming crisis makes it a perfect candidate for exploring the value of CLS-driven leadership. Here's what Jennie Clinton had to say about leading when it matters most.

Q: What crisis challenge or opportunity is of most interest to your organization?

A: I'm focused more and more on unique crisis events such as the pandemic and the increasing number of political disruptions affecting employees and customers. Also, climate change is having a broad-reaching global impact. It's not just a wildfire anymore. It's many wildfires all at once with longer impact.

Q: What specific question(s) do you have regarding your organization's ability to address crisis?

A: My primary questions revolve around the ability to scale. How do we deal with long-term global events? How do we figure out new ways of scaling? How do we engage all of the parts of the organization and have a broader look? How do we move past traditionally defined crisis teams so we can deal with complex issues dealing with our people, customers, and supply chains?

Q: What specific expectations do you have about what's influencing your organization's ability to address crisis?

A: I'm interested in the ability to augment traditional crisis response models with cross-functional, global teams to deal with complexity. The ability to address complexity is a very influential factor regarding crisis management and leadership. We need new crisis impact models which can respond to complex, interdependent events playing out systemically, not just siloed scenarios in one part of the whole. It's necessary to find and tackle the underlying systemic problem in every crisis using cross-functional, global teams. We can then work to address the 10–15% of an event that is specific to a particular crisis with specialists. This allows us to pivot from traditionally defined crisis teams to agile teams configured for complexity. Relatedly, I'm focused on how to get the right people in the right place to respond at scale as well as understanding how crisis events affect everybody in the system.

Q: What sort of information led you to these expectations (e.g., professional journals, expert advice, experience, intuition)?

A: I rely on the entire breadth and depth of talent in Microsoft from data scientists and health specialists to software engineers and social scientists to address the various crises a company our size will encounter. Also, many years of experience and knowing who I can call for advice has helped me to refine my focus on managing complexity. I also look at research on emerging threats and search for new voices and technology so we can adapt. Fresh voices help me explore new ways of doing. We also use debriefing and other forms of knowledge-sharing to learn from crisis events. Finally, we make sure to take a global perspective—not just a US focus—to see the big, systemic picture.

Q: What data and tech are you using to address crisis?

A: As we pivot towards this new, cross-functional model of crisis management, we are using tech that people are familiar with such as Microsoft tools to create a virtual command center. We don't use something new that a person has to learn during crisis. Instead, we stick with available and familiar tools. As things move forward, we see VR and metaverse command centers playing a role. For example, immersive tech that gets you on the ground rapidly without needing to be there physically because it's dangerous or flights are shut down helps maintain an important stream of information during crisis. Similarly, we are also using data sources to track crisis impact in real time. This real-time data tracking on a global scale allows us to make more informed decisions. Finally, we are working to get young tech professionals such as data scientists familiar with crisis so they can improve our ability to make data-informed decisions.

Q: What drove your data and tech choices (e.g., personal decision, team decision, data scientist decision, using what's available, some sort of systematic process for selecting data and tech)?

A: We obviously have our own Microsoft tools, and within this suite of tools, our engineers and product developers help us to understand what applications are (a) comfortable for the user and (b) necessary to implement for addressing our crisis leadership needs.

Q: What sort of data and/or tech are you using to track the impact of your crisis leadership initiatives over time?

A: We have several different layers of response teams and consistently look at lessons learned regarding readiness, training, and why one team performed differently from another over time. We use various points of temporal data to analyze performance response across the organization and why. We dig down to the why so we can incorporate this knowledge into systematic learning.

Q. What sort of data and/or tech are you using to track the impact of your crisis leadership initiatives at multiple levels?

A: We leverage data that helps us understand impacts from events. For example, in COVID-19 we were able to track CDC and WHO data to understand how severe the deaths and outbreaks were in different countries to understand if conditions were favorable to continuing to work from home or start returning to the office. Another example would be tracking the path of a hurricane to gain awareness around what could potentially be impacted at various levels of the organization.

Q: What sort of data and/or tech are you using to track DEI aspects of your crisis leadership initiatives?

A: Our crisis management teams are diverse. As stated earlier, we operate in many countries. Having multi faceted views and expertise when creating these teams is a key factor in our response efforts. For example, we need to consider factors such as global and community cultures, access to resources, and geographic risks (e.g., earthquakes, hurricanes). We can then adapt crisis responses accordingly. Keeping cultural awareness top of mind and how that may impact response and recovery is critical.

Q: What is the (expected) outcome of your tech-enabled plans for crisis leadership?

A: We will increase our flexibility in thinking with data-informed decision-making. Intuition is always part of things, but data and tech drives clarity and alignment in the fog of crisis and provides necessary decision support. You can leverage the data and tech to see what is really happening. You need this data and tech approach to handle the complexity of events. It will allow us to make data-driven decisions. We didn't always have that clarity in the past. Information is often hard to come by in a crisis and technology advances provide us with more data to leverage for crisis response.

Concluding Thoughts about My Interview with Jennie Clinton

I'm impressed by Microsoft's reassuring focus on developing cross-functional, global teams to address the complex and interdependent nature of modern crisis events. It's also compelling that the company enlists engineers and product developers to match tools with needs. Essentially, Microsoft is pivoting toward a systemic approach to managing crisis that will likely drive digital innovations to accommodate this shift. This is similar to architects wanting to create entirely novel skyscrapers—and engineers thus developing equally novel solutions so as to turn that vision into reality. The subsequent suite of tools will represent a fundamental shift in how leaders build global teams and overcome threats to their employees, customers, and supply chains. This emerging tech will significantly increase the pace, power, and scale of collective problem-solving, and CLS-driven leaders who are able to leverage these tools will skyrocket their organizations' preparedness and resilience.

CHAPTER 6

Cultivating Healthy Growth with Healthy People

Health, as the United Nations puts it, is everyone's business. No matter your status, where you are on the planet, your profession, or any other demographic you can think of, at some point in your life health and well-being will play a major role. They're quite simply apex priorities, so it's essential to find new ways to foster positive outcomes in a changing world.

Given that leaders have an exceptional ability to influence outcomes, they need to take charge and move past pre-pandemic initiatives, such as onsite gyms in an offsite world. They need to use data and tech to boost employee health and well-being "anywhere, anytime." This is an opportunity to create and leverage a robust and flexible workforce to outmaneuver and outpace the competition. It's also a grand opportunity to improve the quality of life of billions of people around the globe, which is the highest goal any leader can strive for in business and society.

This chapter explores how you can succeed with all of the above using computational leadership science (CLS). As with the previous chapters, we'll first have a look at what we know (and don't know), this time about creating a happier and healthier society. We'll then cover innovative ways you can take your effectiveness to the next level. Finally, we'll have a look at my Q&A with John Whyte, the Chief Medical Officer of WebMD. He shared several ways leaders can use CLS to improve employee health and well-being.

WHAT WE KNOW ABOUT EMPLOYEE HEALTH AND WELL-BEING

First and foremost, we know the entire world cares about health and well-being. It's a factor at play in all levels of society, from large international organizations down to an individual sitting at a desk writing a book. Here are some concrete examples to put this scale of concern in perspective.

> WORLD INSTITUTIONS ARE CONCERNED. The United Nations identifies ongoing COVID-19 response and recovery as a top priority. It also notes the pandemic has "cast the importance of people-centric health systems into sharp relief." In the same report, it also highlights the continued need to work on "poverty reduction, the promise of leaving no one behind, and the SDGs [Sustainable Development Goals]" to overcome the continued issues with access to essential health services.[1]
>
> The World Health Organization has "Triple Billion" health targets and a public dashboard to track global, regional, and country-level progress. In focusing on "timely, reliable, [and] actionable data," they want to see:
>
> • One billion more people benefiting from universal health coverage;
>
> • One billion more people better protected from health emergencies; and
>
> • One billion more people enjoying better health and well-being.[2,3]
>
> GOVERNMENT LEADERS ARE CONCERNED. They're also united in their message to focus on better health outcomes for all. The G20 formed the Joint Finance and Health Task Force for G20 finance and health ministries to collaborate on prevention, preparedness, and response. From New Zealand and Singapore to Canada, the UAE, the UK, the US, and everywhere in between, countries have health care as a major priority in both their immediate and long-term horizons.[4,5,6,7,8,9]

COMMUNITY LEADERS ARE CONCERNED. Around the world, these leaders are focused on all aspects of public health and well-being. In a large nationwide survey of US school superintendents, 89% "somewhat or strongly agree that schools have a responsibility to provide students with access to mental health care." Religious organizations also work actively with local leaders to promote public health. For example, in the lead-up to Ramadan during the pandemic, the Islamic Advisory Group—an international group focused on "priority health issues among local communities"—worked with local leaders to help community members promote "public health and social measures during the festivities to protect themselves and their loved ones from infection."[10,11]

BUSINESS LEADERS ARE CONCERNED. The Kaiser Family Foundation surveyed executives at over 300 hundred large employers in the US, and an overwhelming majority were either "moderately" (49%), "considerably" (28%), or "strongly" (6%) concerned with the excessive cost of health benefits, with 87% thinking the cost of providing health care to employees will become unsustainable in the next 5 to 10 years. Outside of cost, business leaders are generally concerned with the overall health and well-being of society. Tech giants such as Google, Meta, and Microsoft all have some sort of "for good" program for leveraging their computing power, data, and technical expertise to combat health-related issues. And companies are introducing employee health and wellness services, including nutrition apps, massage therapy, and online mental health programs.[12,13,14,15,16,17]

GRASSROOTS LEADERS ARE CONCERNED. These dedicated individuals form a backstop when formal leadership fails to deliver. An extreme example is the emergence of "governance without (central) government" in the favelas and among the Indigenous communities of Brazil during the pandemic. Former President Jair Bolsonaro's poor handling of COVID-19 created catastrophic health outcomes—especially in marginalized communities—which drove informal networks of leadership to make up for Bolsonaro's shortcomings. It was the bright side of an otherwise dark moment in Brazilian history.[18]

Collectively, from grassroot challenges up to global threats, the silver lining is that leaders have more data than ever before to increase health and well-being. The key is understanding what health leadership is and how it can apply reams of data to drive radical advancements in care, safety, and wellness in organizations.

DEFINING MODERN HEALTH AND WELL-BEING LEADERS AND LEADERSHIP

I define *health leadership* as a *process* for leveraging health care products and services to provide high-quality, sustainable, equitable, and inclusive health and well-being programs for diverse employees. One example would be a leadership process that's able to anticipate dips in employee mental health and swiftly intervene with digital coaching to avoid a staffing crisis.[19]

Relatedly, a *health leader* is an *individual* who's able to connect people, distribute tasks, and sustain necessary levels of motivation to set these processes in motion. One example would be a leader engaging experts and stakeholders to decide (a) which digital tools are best for supporting employee mental health, and (b) how to promote their use throughout the organization.

The effectiveness of leaders and leadership to achieve such outcomes is important at every level of business and society. There's arguably no bigger threat to economies, employers, and employees than factors related to health and well-being. Consider these eye-watering examples.

GLOBAL HEALTH AND WELL-BEING IS AT STAKE. Keeping the public healthy keeps economies growing. Unfortunately, the CDC notes that noncommunicable diseases (NCDs)—including heart disease, cancer, chronic respiratory disease, and diabetes—are the leading cause of death worldwide, killing 41 million people each year. That's a whopping 70% of deaths worldwide! The WHO, building on these worrying statistics, points out that "almost the entire global population (99%) breaths air that exceeds WHO air quality limits and threatens their health."[20,21]

POOR GLOBAL HEALTH IS COSTLY AND IT'S GOING TO LIMIT PRODUC-TIVITY. Research appearing in *The Lancet Public Health* esti-mated health care spending in the US alone related to "modifiable risk factors" such as high body-mass index, dietary risks, and tobacco smoke was $730.4 billion in one year. Essentially, the cost of preventable risk in *just* the US is equiva-lent to the GDP of all but 19 of the richest countries in the world. And no matter how bad it is in so-called developed counties, low-income nations have it far worse. They have to manage unbelievably extreme health-related threats with very small budgets. Even though health care spending has doubled from 2000 to 2019 (now making up 10% of global GDP), only 20% of that spending was in low-income nations. This sys-temic inequality leads to a health care system where the major-ity of health costs are paid out-of-pocket (44%) and an economic base with zero slack to withstand shocks such as pan-demics or the effects of climate change. So, from the richest countries to the poorest countries, businesses are faced with extreme risk, where unhealthy lifestyles and broken health care systems will translate into extreme absenteeism, turnover, and other major employee issues if leaders don't act now.[22,23,24]

SOARING HEALTH CARE COSTS ARE OVERWHELMING EMPLOYERS. According to the US Bureau of Labor Statistics, employer costs in the US for employee health insurance now makes up 7.1% of total compensation costs on average in the private sector and 11.2% in the public sector. This "compensation component" is one of the largest reported costs, only outpaced by "wages and salaries." And it's unsurprisingly a major con-cern for employers: The Kaiser Family Foundation surveyed over 300 US leaders from large private companies, and the majority (86%) reported a need for increased government involvement to contain costs and to ensure employee health.[25,26]

Indeed, researchers and practitioners are calling for changes to the role of health leadership in business and society. The goal is to cre-ate a holistic approach to encouraging and training a new breed of leaders and establishing entirely new structures to ensure that employee health and well-being remains a priority. Leaders will need to expand their capacity, encourage stakeholders to change, and drive modifications to the systems. Accomplishing this multilevel mission with CLS will create next-level leaders who can facilitate a digitally supported environment where stakeholders collectively make unprecedented shifts in health and well-being.[27,28]

The ability to establish such a fundamentally positive shift as a CLS-driven leader is an amazing legacy to leave. Here are some recommendations for leaders beginning their own digital transformation.

LEADERS NEED TO APPRECIATE INFORMATION TECHNOLOGY. We know that health leaders with IT-related skills and IT project-management experience are more likely to establish broad stakeholder adoption of health information technology. As I mentioned in a March 2022 *Harvard Business Review* article, "This does not mean you have to code in Python, but you must at least dip your toe in the digital water." Easing into this pool of opportunity is crucial for delivering better employee outcomes.[29,30]

LEADERS NEED VISION AND A PROACTIVE DRIVE FOR DIGITAL TRANSFORMATION. A good start would be to actively form partnerships with leaders such as chief medical information officers and chief health officers as well as institutions promoting digital transformation. The Cleveland Clinic, for example, has "Cleveland Clinic Employer Solutions" to help leaders implement innovative tools for improving employee health and well-being. Case studies repeatedly find that leaders increase their digital transformation effectiveness when they establish strong ties with these technical allies. They help illuminate the full value of connecting technological advancements with employee outcomes.[31,32]

Also, if you're one of these IT experts, remember to help others feel comfortable with digital transformation—in fact, that's where your leadership challenge lies. Many of the barriers to transformation stem from unfamiliarity, fear, and skepticism based on incomplete information. This problem will not go away; it will likely increase given the speed of innovation in the health sector. As a digital steward, you'll need to ensure that stakeholders keep pace with change to secure buy-in.

LEADERS NEED TO APPRECIATE PROCESSES. The next step after establishing oneself as a well-rounded, CLS-driven leader is to set up broader leadership processes. Researchers have identified seven themes for effectively guiding a digital transformation process:

- Communicate clear visions and goals;

- Provide leadership support;

- Establish a governance structure;

- Establish training;

- Identify and appoint champions;

- Address work-process change; and

- Follow up.[33]

These are important steps because leadership has to manage an ever-increasing number of interrelated challenges connecting traditionally siloed experts. One challenge might call for a leadership process configured to incorporate epidemiologists, virologists, and social psychologists to overcome vaccine hesitancy among employees. Another challenge could require the same process to stream in information from accountants, economists, and occupational therapists to develop the best plan for providing cost-effective, safe workstations for employees working at home. An effective leadership process—guided by an effective leader—rapidly adapts to meet these emerging needs. That adaptive fulfillment of needs improves stakeholder cohesion and sense of empowerment, helps with cost containment, and ultimately improves employee health and well-being outcomes.[34]

LEADERS NEED TO APPRECIATE DATA PRIVACY AND SECURITY. Since health leaders deal with extremely sensitive employee data, they need to develop cybersecurity policies and practices, provide cybersecurity-awareness training programs, and make large (visible) investments in their cybersecurity programs so as to establish trust with employees. Leaders in general need to develop strategies for handling the large amounts of data they're accumulating. They need to think of ways of turning employee health and well-being data into actionable insights— while ensuring their organizations are compliant with privacy laws and regulations. In short, employee health and well-being data is a double-edged sword: those who proactively lead with it will drive innovative solutions; those who reactively manage it expose their organizations to substantial risk.

Leaders need to appreciate proactive and systemic approaches to employee health and well-being. Modern leaders also need to focus more on preventative care. Both employers and employees need to increase their understanding of proactive factors such as nutrition, exercise, and mental health. Modern health and well-being systems in action also need to establish a holistic approach where information flows freely and securely across silos to provide better service throughout an employee's journey. As I will discuss in the section on CLS-relevant technologies, there are several digital innovations for speeding up the transitions from reaction-oriented leadership to prevention-oriented health and well-being. But before that, let's first consider some of the worrying blind spots in business and society's understanding of health and well-being.[35]

What We Don't Know about Employee Health and Well-being

The promise of the digital transformation and overall reform of health care is exciting, but there are still many unknowns.

Health care leaders, particularly those coming up through medical school, often lack formal training in leadership competencies. This blind spot is a major concern because it inhibits medical experts' ability to connect with the outside world and put their knowledge into de-siloed action.[36]

Though larger organizations have in-house chief medical officers and other health-related professionals to connect the dots, many smaller organizations cannot make this investment—which limits their ability to achieve next-level employee health and well-being. Practitioners and researchers, therefore, need to develop strategies so an increasing number of medical experts can effectively engage with business and society. Fortunately, as I will discuss in the next section, organizations such as the American Association for Physician Leadership (AAPL), the American Society of Anesthesiologists Center for Physician Leadership Excellence (ASA-CPLE), and the Mayo Clinic are generating data-driven insights that leaders can use to boost employee health and well-being.[37,38,39]

THERE'S ALSO AN INSUFFICIENT UNDERSTANDING OF HOW LEADER-SHIP SHAPES EMPLOYEE HEALTH AND WELL-BEING OVER TIME. Experts are unable to accurately predict how changes to leadership styles or structures, as well as leader traits and behaviors, will influence an organization's ability to digitally transform and deliver better-quality health and well-being products and services. For example, though distributed leadership processes and cooperative leaders will likely drive employee-centered change to health and well-being, this is only speculation; we'll need multiple streams of longitudinal data to support such claims.

WE ALSO KNOW LITTLE ABOUT THE LEADERSHIP PROCESSES NECESSARY FOR CONNECTING STRATEGIC-LEVEL DECISIONS WITH FRONTLINE ATTITUDES, BELIEFS, NORMS, AND BEHAVIOR. The pace of digital transformation, for instance, calls for mid-level leaders to manage the disconnect between strategical-level expectations and frontline-employee realities. Likewise, these mid-level leaders must manage frontline expectations regarding support from senior leadership. This blind spot between expected pace at the top and expected resources at the frontline is one of the main reasons why digital transformations can fail. Employers and employees have respective doubts regarding ability and support, and those doubts inhibit growth. I'll next discuss how you can use your CLS toolbox to bridge this gap and accelerate the digital maturity of your organization.

FINALLY, WE DON'T KNOW IF DECISION-MAKERS WILL FULLY EMBRACE A DIGITAL FUTURE. Though leaders with existing IT skills and IT project-management experience are more likely to develop the long-term vision necessary for successful digital transformation, it's unclear if the reverse is true: whether visionary leaders lacking an IT background will innately seek out the technical training necessary for driving change. Assuming they have the motivation to proactively address their technical deficits could lead to major disruptions resulting from leader hesitancy, procrastination, and fear.[40]

Such blind spots represent an inability to channel floods of data into usable rivers of knowledge. Fortunately, many CLS-relevant tools are available to harness this untapped energy.

CLS-RELEVANT TECHNOLOGY FOR REMOVING BLIND SPOTS AND LEADING TRANSFORMATION

In this section, I'll discuss some of the innovations emerging in health care and how your health and well-being initiatives can dovetail these advancements. The goal is inspiring cross-functional ideas and opportunities for proactive collaboration between health care providers and employers. To start building this bridge, I'll discuss how data and tech can inspire personal development, then interpersonal development, and finally systemic development.

Leadership Challenge: Improving Training and Development

As I touched on earlier, there are several data-driven assessment tools health care institutions are using to gain a better understanding of a leader's strengths and opportunities for improvement. The Mayo

Clinic Leader Index, for example, is a valuable tool for understanding how others perceive a leader's capabilities in a health care setting. The AAPL's Physician-Mapped Leadership Assessment and Development Tool provides physicians with insights regarding both their unique leader profile and how the results map on to specific physician leadership competencies. Finally, the ASA-CPLE's development assessments are data-driven tools based on a suite of Hogan Personality Solutions. These are proven solutions for developing talent based on the "big five" personality traits: openness to experience, conscientiousness, extraversion, agreeableness, and neuroticism. The assessment highlights physician-specific strengths as well as opportunities for improvement.[41,42]

Decision-makers working with data scientists and personality experts can use this seemingly disconnected, physician-oriented data to help leaders refine their ability to promote employee health and well-being. For example, personality research shows that high-performing clinicians such as surgeons tend to be more conscientious and more emotionally stable. This profile allows them to stay highly focused on their patient's health while managing the stress of this responsibility. You can use such insights to customize leadership training. Some leaders might score high on conscientiousness and low on emotional stability. This means they'll likely engage deeply with employee well-being, but they may also obsessively focus on the needs of others and burn themselves out in the process. Leaders fitting this profile will benefit from training that helps them to process difficult emotions, manage stress, and maintain composure. On the other hand, leaders might score low on conscientiousness and high on emotional stability. These individuals may need training to increase their reliability in helping employees with health and well-being issues. They can accomplish this task by (a) creating a playbook for handling various employee needs and (b) making detailed to-do lists to track their progress.[43]

The main point is that our ability to leverage data across boundaries is rapidly expanding. You can incorporate any number of variables to predict the likelihood of a leader significantly improving employee health and well-being. In addition to utilizing personality data, you can stream in subjective 360° ratings on a leader's ability to promote health and well-being. You can also leverage the objective data from a leader's team, including number of sick days and vacation days used, task completion rates, and turnover. Data scientists can then help you use this data to precisely identify what leaders can do—from working on their emotional stability to encouraging the use of vacation days—to boost employee health and well-being. Decision-makers arriving at this confluence of data, tech, and analytical expertise will extract game-changing insights for cultivating healthy growth with healthy people.

Leadership Challenge: Improving Leadership Processes

Leaders also need to construct effective leadership processes for sustaining employee health and well-being. Following are three CLS examples for turbocharging your efforts.

> TELEHEALTH: One way the health sector is addressing the needs of patients is by providing them with a deeper sense of confidence and security. To provide this sense of safety, organizations are developing "anytime, anywhere" telehealth solutions. No matter where patients are, or when they seek attention, a personalized team will be available. Offering the latest in telehealth empowers employees and it demonstrates your 24/7 commitment to health and well-being.

> AUGMENTED AND VIRTUAL REALITY: The health sector is also addressing the needs of its staff by helping them establish familiarity with potentially high-risk medical procedures in low-risk, practice environments. Health care companies are developing sophisticated products based on augmented reality (or "AR": seeing virtual elements in the physical world) and virtual reality (or "VR": being fully immersed in a virtual world) to train and empower the next generation of physicians. Early results already show an increase in physician performance of high-risk procedures with significantly reduced risk to the patient.[44]

> Here, again, you can adopt advancements in the health sector to improve the health and well-being of your employees.

Rather than focusing on the corporate gym, for example, subsidize the latest in VR fitness to engage many more employees than a centralized facility could—especially now that many employees work remotely. Jay Croft from WebMD shares the following about VR fitness: "For people who have never exercised, it can be a bridge to healthier lifestyles. For people who have limited ability to leave the home—because of age or a medical condition—it can be life-changing." In addition to physical fitness, you can also provide your employees with on-demand VR services to proactively address anxiety, depression, and stress. Employees can even take a virtual swim with dolphins to manage their physical pain. Ultimately, whatever you choose to invest in, it has to be something that employees will use to improve their health and well-being. Getting this selection process right unlocks the full potential of digital transformation for cultivating healthy growth with healthy people.[45,46,47]

SWARM INTELLIGENCE. The "digital swarm intelligence" I introduced in Chapter 2 takes distributed leadership to the next level with real-time collective decision-making. The platforms—based on algorithms of swarming behavior found in nature—allow a connected network of stakeholders using their desktops or mobile devices to repeatedly swipe toward a preferred choice on their screen, such as a preferred digital tool for mental health. The underlying AI then "swarms" to a collective outcome based on factors such as the intensity and frequency of individual swipes. This CLS-driven approach boosts your understanding of what stakeholders want in terms of health and well-being services—and thus what you should subsequently invest in. Using swarm tech allows you to achieve real-time consensus-making, so you don't have to deal with the lag associated with surveys. It also drastically reduces the biases that limit the input of lower-ranked yet no less knowledgeable individuals. For example, you can rapidly find out what types of telehealth services your employees prefer without worrying that the decisions are being driven by the loudest person in the room. This is a great example of how CLS-driven leaders create employee-centered leadership processes: they increase employee engagement while decreasing the likelihood of investing in unwanted health and well-being offerings.[48]

Systemic Challenge: Improving the Overall Health and Well-being System

Finally, before you can ascend as a CLS-driven leader in a futuristic leadership process, you have to put your head down and focus on the foundational work. This requires a health and well-being system fundamentally rooted in data that is secure and interoperable. Simply put, there is no flashy future if you cannot safely and consistently share data. Without going into too much detail, data leads to information, and information leads to the beneficial knowledge digital transformations have to offer. It's your responsibility as a CLS-driven leader to ensure this journey from data to digital transformation happens with minimal cost and maximum benefit. Here are a few ideas to help you on your way.

To start with the moonshot, my first choice would be an interoperable, inter-organizational, privacy-preserving health and well-being platform that all organizations could connect to and learn from. But this idea hinges on the ability to securely share standardized data. Practitioners and researchers would need access to interoperable data for improved detection and mitigation of threats to employee health and well-being—from chronic work-related stress to the next major public health crisis. Increased levels of data- and information-sharing are critical for creating this holistic, employee-center ecosystem. Various methods for collecting and sharing data—such as health records, fitness-app data, and HR data related to sick leave—will need to work in unison for better anticipation of needs, specialized interventions, and faster and more accurate treatment.[49]

Once business and society has this foundational work complete (or at least it's heading in the right direction), then we can properly move to the flashy work of digital transformation. Here are two examples of this exciting future:

- Leaders with a strong understanding of digital systems—utilizing the Internet of Things, AI, VR, and the growing plethora of other digital innovations—would be enabled to offer "digital human" assistants that provide highly personalized employee support. These AI-powered digital humans plugged into sophisticated chatbots such as ChatGPT could work like an all-in-one companion, dietician, personal trainer, and therapist.[50]

- Leaders creating opportunities for sharing data and information among organizations would be able to incorporate AI-supported platforms to instantly find the right people for the right job. For example, let's say an employee has a unique set of medical conditions; such a system could rapidly identify the health-care providers best suited to help. It could even search across organizations in a privacy-preserving manner to find others with similar health concerns. Provided that both parties consent to identifying themselves, they could connect to offer each other moral support and share best practices for living and working with their medical conditions.

Though much of this latter section on improving the overall health and well-being system is still very much blue-sky dreaming, momentum is heading in this direction. Most large tech companies already rely on hyper-connected, large-scale networks of people and machines working together to rapidly develop, find, and share knowledge. So it's only a matter of time until this "augmented collective intelligence" works its way into systems for improving employee health and well-being. I know much of this seems far off, but taking steps today to prepare for this transformation—such as introducing digital-swarm platforms for boosting collective decision-making—will make a huge difference in the long-term health and well-being of both your employees and your organization as a whole.[51]

As it happens, my Q&A with the Chief Medical Officer of WebMD confirmed this assessment. Following is what he had to say regarding opportunities for leaders to leverage data and tech in the pursuit of a happier and healthier workforce.

EMPLOYEE HEALTH AND WELL-BEING Q&A WITH WEBMD

"I want to see democratized services and information as well as leaders using data to understand what really makes a difference when it comes to employee health and well-being."
— *John Whyte, Chief Medical Officer, WebMD*

To discuss the value of relevant data and tech, I spoke with Dr. John Whyte, the Chief Medical Officer of WebMD—the leading online publisher of resources pertaining to health and well-being.

WebMD reaches more visitors than any other private or government health-related website does: it receives a staggering 130 million unique visitors per month, who view 230 million pages per month. Simply put, it's the go-to place for trustworthy and timely medical news and information—and so Dr. Whyte is the logical choice to interview about health and well-being. Now let's see what he had to say.

Q. What health and well-being challenges or opportunities do you think are of most interest to leaders?

A: Health is everyone's business. Health happens outside of the hospital and the doctor's office. Keeping costs under control and having a productive workforce are important opportunities moving forward. Business and society need to pivot towards new ways of addressing employee health. Finally, organizations need to address mental health in addition to physical health.

Q: What specific questions do you have about a leader's ability to address health and well-being in the workplace?

A: I'm interested in how leaders set long-term commitment. I want to know if they'll stick to these long-term commitments once they recognize that some changes will have short-term costs, and I want to know how they'll managing the financial costs. In addition, I want to know how leaders are measuring employee expectations, and what are the best ways to understand employee needs.

Q: What specific expectations do you have about what's influencing a leader's ability to address health and well-being in the workplace?

A: Employee turnover is influencing employer behavior. People will simply look for better employee benefits elsewhere if their current employer isn't constantly improving. Leaders have to show how they are addressing employee interests regarding health and well-being. Another major influence is transparency. Leaders have to demonstrate that they're walking the talk.

Q: What sort of information led you to these expectations (e.g., professional journals, expert advice, experience, intuition)?

A: I rely on surveys of companies, data about industry, data about my own company, Bureau of Labor Statistics data, and general economic data. I'm about the data. That said, I also like to listen to what leaders and employees are saying.

Q: What data and tech do you recommend for addressing employee health and well-being?

A: First, I recommend making tech available to employees. It's not just about the office gym. Leaders can offer reimbursement for mental health apps, make available continuous glucose monitoring sensors, or pay for tech such as Lumen to improve metabolic efficiency. Essentially, it's not about any particular tool. Leaders, instead, need to recognize they can help their employees with advancements in tech.

Q: What drives your data and tech recommendations (e.g., personal experience, advice from technical and subject matter experts, some sort of systematic process for selecting data and tech)?

A: I use data to look at trends in tech, and I rely on my experience regarding changes to health and wellness initiatives in the workplace over the years.

Q: What data and tech can leaders use to analyze the impact of their health and well-being initiatives over time?

A: They can use continuous and systematic surveys with methodological rigor. They can rely on temporal data to look at absenteeism, early retirement, quitting, and firing. They can then overlay the data to look at trends relative to changes in health and well-being initiatives over time. The key is structing the data, ensuring data integrity, and bringing it all together.

Q: What data and tech can leaders use to analyze the impact of their health and well-being initiatives at multiple levels (e.g., individual, team, department, and so on)?

A: Leaders can use data similar to my answer for the previous question. Leaders can also explore how many employees have used all of their vacation days—and if not, why. Individuals, teams, departments, or even the entire organization could be overworking. If that's the case, then leaders need to commit to cultural change. For example, they can turn off emails after hours and ensure that people are using their paid time off to recharge.

Q: What data and tech can employers use to measure DEI (diversity, equity, and inclusion) factors as part of their health and well-being initiatives?

A: First, stakeholders need to hold leaders accountable. When I was at the FDA, I ensured a very diverse team, and that was a conscious effort for achieving a diverse representation. At WebMD, I literally pushed to find new and diverse images for webpages. Like a big jigsaw puzzle, everyone plays a role. Leaders also need to run demographics pertaining to health and well-being, make the data visible, and make it clear that there's true anonymity for employees when it comes to sharing concerns.

Q: What are the (expected) outcomes of data and tech-enabled initiatives for employee health and well-being?

A: I want to see democratized services and information as well as leaders using data to understand what really makes a difference when it comes to employee health and well-being. I also want to see standardized processes and creating a loop where info goes in, it's then analyzed, refined, incorporated, and fed back into analysis. Emerging tech is allowing leaders to do much more of that—in a structured way. It needs to continue and pick up pace.

Concluding Thoughts about My Interview with John Whyte

Dr. Whyte is data driven and person centered. He focused on the importance of improving employee health and well-being with data and tech because it's both the right thing to do and because it offers a competitive advantage. He made it clear that, moving forward, leaders will need to adopt this data-driven, person-centered focus to get the best out of people. Remember, health care is now everyone's business, and great leaders will use the latest data and tech to establish a resilient workforce. In other words, leveraging CLS to improve employee health and well-being sets the bar high when it comes to attracting and retaining top talent.

As a final note, I want to take a moment and thank every health care professional as well as the unseen and frequently unpaid heroes providing tireless care to loved ones. Business and society would come to a standstill if it wasn't for this huge network of both professional and informal care. They provide mission-critical services to us all. It's this sort of passion and dedication that I hope will drive you to innovative groundbreaking solutions. Dig deep into CLS, and I promise you'll have the tools to improve the health and well-being of all those around you.

PART II

BEING ABOUT COMPUTATIONAL LEADERSHIP

CHAPTER 7

Becoming a Digital Golf Pro and Growing Digital Trees

Computational leadership science (CLS) is more than just addressing the six strategic priorities I covered in the previous chapters. Rather, it's a universal tool delivering game-changing results in any situation. Accordingly, I'm going to provide you with a detailed and easy-to-use set of instructions for configuring CLS to suit your specific leadership needs.

In this chapter, we'll first explore how you can benefit from hiring a CLS advisor—an expert who can blend data and tech with social and behavioral sciences to improve leadership outcomes. CLS advisors can help you navigate your personal voyage of data and digital transformation. They guide you to a place where your leadership experience and intuition is boosted with the latest in science and technology. CLS advisors essentially help you remain competitive in an environment where digital tools are must-haves.

Then I'll introduce a simple hack for addressing the complexity of leading in the age of digital transformation—what I call the "CLS Priority Matrix." At the root of most (if not all) high-level priorities are one of two systemic challenges, and the CLS Priority Matrix sets the foundation for lasting change. You'll go from tending to each individual leaf and branch of your organization to instead nurturing the whole system. After that, I'll touch on how to build CLS-driven teams and then leverage their cross-functional strength for unmatched performance.

Four Questions for Selecting a CLS Advisor

CLS—the "intersection of trailblazing science and technology, well-established leadership research, and invaluable knowledge gleaned from practice"—is fundamentally improving leadership. Leaders arriving at the CLS intersection are making and saving their organizations billions while driving unprecedented levels of innovation.[1]

Finding this sweet spot, however, is not easy. Technological advancements are rapid and complex, and building a CLS team is time-consuming. This is where an advisor can help you leverage the full power of CLS. They work like a highly skilled golf pro guiding you through the digital course of transformation. They know the course better than most do and can advise on which digital club you should use in every situation. They're behind the scenes helping you take world-class shots.

If you're interested in engaging with a CLS advisor (which I'm assuming you are), then here are four critical questions for selecting the right person:

How can you help me overcome my biases?

Your CLS advisor must understand the difference between your needs and your wants. For example, leaders *need* to increase diversity, equity, and inclusion (DEI), but research shows they tend to hire people they *want* based on subconscious biases related to socioeconomic background, a preference for extraverts, and other counterproductive factors.[2]

Have a look at the "cognitive bias codex" at commons.wikimedia.org to get an idea of just how many biases leaders need to overcome. These biases affect everything from homogenous hiring and promotion to the formation of fragile, just-in-time supply chains.[3,4,5]

A good CLS advisor helps you separate needs from wants so you can effectively apply your CLS intelligence. A good CLS advisor also knows how to incorporate emerging technology to accelerate your debiasing process. Microsoft and Thomson Reuters, for example, are developing "knowledge graphs"—large, complex networks of information—to help leaders broaden their search space and avoid tunnel vision when making strategic decisions.[6,7]

Tip: Before meeting with a potential advisor, first review resources such as the cognitive bias codex and other readily available materials to get an idea of what's out there regarding human biases. This will help you gauge their understanding of the topic.

How can you help me frame my needs with leadership science?

Your CLS advisor must grasp traditional leadership science as well as advancements in research. This is important because emerging challenges and opportunities require a radical rethinking of our go-to tools. For example, blending natural sciences with leadership studies has led to the emergence of an evolution-based understanding of leadership. CLS advisors using this theoretical framework apply the dynamics of (cultural) evolution—that is, variation, selection, and retention of successful traits—to better understand leadership practices and how to orchestrate purposeful change. They also incorporate various (computational) methods to help you model, predict, and guide your success. And they draw upon proven CLS practices such as Apple's "evolutionary design model" for driving innovation.[8,9]

Tip: Again, prior to any meeting, spend 5–10 minutes researching the history of leadership science so you can better assess the advisor's understanding of this complex phenomenon.

How can you help me explore my needs?

Your CLS advisor must also have familiarity with qualitative and quantitative research methods. Certain needs, such as morale, are perhaps better understood from a qualitative perspective because close-ended questions gloss over the thoughts and feelings of staff. In one case, J.D. Power used "sentiment analysis" of employee Facebook posts at Delta Air Lines to help the airline improve employee experiences during COVID-19. The result—as explained by Michael Rambus, Program Manager of Global Employee Engagement at Delta—is that they gained an invaluable feature utilized on a daily basis.[10]

Conversely, asking employees open-ended questions about DEI and other loaded topics leads to the bias mentioned earlier, where people report a more positive perception of reality compared to the "ground truth" of objective data. This is why companies such as ADP and institutions such as MIT are developing diversity dashboards. The tech can undercover hidden patterns of inequality in quantitative data so that leaders can make lasting change. A good CLS advisor knows how to put you down this ground-truth path.[11,12]

Finally, it is important to note there's no one way for exploring your needs. Your CLS advisor has to help you balance deep qualitative insights with the more objective data of quantitative research. For example, leaders at the Silicon Valley corporation Cisco use a combination of methods to achieve industry-leading workforce planning in a tight labor market with extreme competition for top talent. Like the goal of the game Tetris, they quickly find a variety of gaps in their operations and fill them with the appropriate talent. One way Cisco does this is by combining (a) quantitative data regarding key performance indicators of high potential employees with (b) qualitative analysis of leader feedback on what makes someone successful in key strategic roles. This hybrid approach enables the company to rapidly align individual strengths of high potentials with critical needs for growth. Your advisor must help you adopt the same approach so you can address your priorities with agility *and* accuracy.[13]

> *Tip: Have a look at—and ask potential advisors about—their track records using qualitative and quantitative methods to address organizational challenges and priorities. You need to avoid intuition-driven advisors who lack the ability to derive actionable insights from this data-rich world.*

How can you help me use computer and data science to get what I need?

Your CLS advisor needs to understand the difference between computer scientists and data scientists, and what can (and cannot) be delivered by these overlapping but different specialists. Data scientists focus primarily on finding insights from data—qualitative and quantitative—using algorithms and deep knowledge in areas such as statistics. Computer scientists, on the other hand, have deep knowledge in all things IT, and they build the data ecosystems that allow data scientists to perform their work.

A good CLS advisor will use this distinction to accelerate your performance. If you need to leverage data insights to increase your effectiveness as a leader of DEI, supply chains, and more, then incorporate data scientists. However, if you need to develop scalable platforms for tasks such as hiring, training and development, and investment management, then computer scientists come into play.

Also, note that using computer and data science is *not* an either/or decision. Large tech firms, including Amazon, Google, and Meta, employ thousands of computer and data scientists to co-create game-changing technology for everything from finance to health care to retail. Your CLS advisor will help you engage these specialists to find insights and build platforms for taking your leadership to the next level.

> *Tip: Your potential CLS advisor doesn't need to be an expert at using every digital club in the bag—that's impossible. Instead, the advisor needs to know what clubs are in the bag, what's good for you, and which specialists can help you use them.*

Collectively, these four questions help you systematically isolate, frame, explore, and address your needs like never before. It's your step-by-step process for finding the right person to help you with personal growth in the digital era.

Admittedly, however, since CLS is an emerging field, we don't yet have access to a formal pool of CLS advisors. In the future you'll likely find "computational leadership scientists" and "leadership technologists," but for now you might have to search for leadership scholars with an interest in computational science or tech-driven experts with an appreciation for leadership science. And, of course, you can get in touch with me for advice on developing a next-level digital culture.

My initial recommendation is that you dive deep into the situational dynamics influencing transformation and growth. It's about seeing the roots of a challenge and growing new opportunities. Here, the metaphor switches from digital golfing to digital gardening.

TWO SYSTEMIC FACTORS FOR GROWING YOUR ORGANIZATION

Large systemic failures are increasing in frequency and intensity. They're disrupting all aspects of business and society and will continue to have catastrophic consequences if leaders don't fundamentally change their behavior. Leaders are at a critical stage where deep, stakeholder-oriented changes—rather than surface-level quick fixes—are a must. The topical (duct tape) approach to leading no longer applies. Instead, there's an urgent need for systemic leaders who incorporate data, behavioral science, and cutting-edge tech to make real change.

To guide you on this journey of resilience and growth, I'm introducing a simplified approach to systemic thinking that combines my CLS Priority Matrix—based on people and sustainability challenges—with an appreciation for a world that is VUCA—volatile, uncertain, complex, and ambiguous.

I'm keeping the framework intentionally simple to avoid pushing people back into their familiar but confining box of intuition. I very much want you to avoid that trap. So, like with any good computational method, we will start off as simply as possible and add complexity when needed. The CLS Priority Matrix and VUCA are starting points. Plans will evolve as you interact with your CLS advisor and the CLS teams you build along the way. I just want you to practice thinking systemically at this stage.

The Systemic Roots

As Kenneth Boulding, one of the founders of general systems theory, timelessly put it, "much valuable information and insights can be obtained by applying low-level systems to high-level subject matter." In other words, the roots of a tree are very important for maintaining and improving the health of its trunk, branches, and leaves. Leaders not getting at the systemic roots of an organization will overlook valuable knowledge and opportunities. They will spend their time fixing one surface level problem after the next. It's akin to taping dying leaves on a tree when the roots need attention.[14]

Fortunately, as noted by Gartner, most high-level strategic priorities—from blockchain to well-being—grow from the systemic roots of people and sustainability factors. This means that chaotic events on the surface—the digital winds of change—are manageable when you tend to the consistent and predictable roots of your organization. For example, a report by McKinsey on cybersecurity during COVID-19 found that many businesses pivoted "from working on routine tasks [the leaves] and toward the long-term goals of establishing secure connections for newly minted remote workforces [the roots]." The pandemic made leaders realize they needed to step away from the day-to-day challenges of cybersecurity and invest in a *sustainable* IT infrastructure capable of handling the major shift in how people work.[15,16]

Similarly, effective leaders realize that *people* issues such as customer service, employee engagement, and well-being improve when the focus is on the systemic roots of human psychology rather than on siloed concerns at the tip of each organizational branch. This is why 83% of "digitally maturing companies" in a recent survey conducted by Deloitte use cross-functional teams. Everyone is empowered to dig deep into a challenge and nurture organizational health from the interconnected source. These leading organizations are finding effective ways to co-create generalizable and systemic solutions to operations. They don't reinvent wheels in isolated departments. Instead, they collectively learn and grow.[17,18]

Nurturing the Roots with Enlightened Attention

The roots of an organization require "enlightened attention" to support growth. Leaders need to know *what* resources are necessary, *when* they're necessary, *why* they're necessary, and *how* much support to allocate to them. Haphazardly adding the organizational equivalent of too much water and nutrients is not enlightened attention—it's a waste of time and money that could kill the tree. This is something great leaders understand and avoid through years of trial and error. They have a knack for seeing patterns of growth and adjusting their strategy to create and maintain a healthy organization.

CLS combines this intuitive knack with proven behavioral science, data, and technology to boost the speed, scale, and sustainability of growth. Regarding the systemic roots of people and sustainability, two behavioral science frameworks are ideal for germinating next-level outcomes (see Figures 7.1a and 7.1b).

Examples of High-Level People Priorities

Talent Management

Employee Engagement

Remote Working

DEI

Systemic-Level People Factors

The CAR root influences all high-level people priorities.

(a)

Examples of High-Level Sustainability Priorities

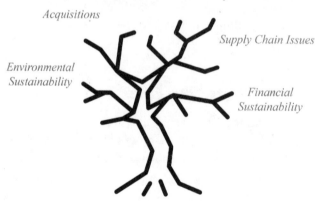

Acquisitions

Supply Chain Issues

Environmental Sustainability

Financial Sustainability

Systemic-Level Sustainability Factors

The EET root influences all high-level sustainability priorities.

(b)

Figures 7.1a and 7.1b   Systemic-level factors and examples of associated high-level priorities.

PEOPLE FACTORS ROOTED IN SELF-DETERMINATION THEORY: This framework focuses on satisfying basic, universal needs for competence, autonomy, and relatedness—that is, CAR-driven needs—to enhance engagement, motivation, well-being, and other priorities related to human psychology.[19]

SUSTAINABILITY FACTORS ROOTED IN THE EXPLORATION-EXPLOITATION TRADE-OFF: This framework focuses on the trade-off between exploiting old certainties versus exploring new opportunities. Understanding how to balance exploration-exploitation trade-offs—that is, EET challenges—is essential for managing ecological concerns, financial investments, and other priorities related to sustainable growth.[20]

The people root is reliable because humans display consistent patterns in how they feel, think, and behave. We can say with relative certainty that individuals are motivated to accept data and digital transformation when it helps them know more about what they want, such as the secrets to a happy and healthy life (competence). Adoption also improves when digital tools allow people to exercise greater control, such as having access to anytime, anywhere HR support in the age of remote working (autonomy), and when innovations deepen supportive partnerships, such as new technologies to improve mentoring programs (relatedness).[21,22,23]

The sustainability root is helpful for understanding the constant tension between exploration and exploitation in organizations. For instance, corporations face EET challenges when they choose between exploring green practices to benefit stakeholders versus exploiting cheaper, unsustainable alternatives to maximize shareholder value, or when they choose between investing in updating critical IT infrastructure versus avoiding the cost of modernizing their systems.

As I'll discuss in the coming sections, you can you use these two proven frameworks to grow any organizational tree—from the SME bonsai to the multinational redwood. CAR and EET allow you to drill down into the systemic roots of your challenges. And they provide you with a common language so a diverse group of experts—from computer scientists to psychologists—can help you cultivate next-level opportunities.

In order to get you these blue-ribbon outcomes, let's first have a look at the roots of your tree. I want you to go past your visible problems and see the underlying drivers of surface-level outcomes. In other words, pick up your shovel. It's time to dig.

Understanding the Roots with Systemic Thinking

Think about a difficult challenge you're currently facing. Score it on a scale of 1 to 5 (with 1 being very much *not* about finding a sustainable balance and 5 being very much about finding a sustainable balance). Now do the same for the people factor (with 1 being very much *not* about people and 5 being very much about people). For example, certain finance issues such as cash flow and capital funding may score very high on organizational sustainability factors and relatively low on people factors, while certain priorities such as bullying in the workplace may score very high on people factors and relatively low on sustainability factors.

Remember, this is an intentionally simplified step to get things started; I know people and sustainability concerns overlap. Just quickly score your priority on these two factors and see where it lands on the CLS Priority Matrix (see Figure 7.2).

The CLS Priority Matrix is a mindset shift, not a solution. I want you to think about the roots below the surface because they're the true starting point for lasting change. Specifically:

- If your high-level challenge scores above three on only sustainability or people, then you have a clear starting point. Congratulations!

- If your challenge scores above three on both sustainability and people, then simplify for now and chose either sustainability or people as the primary concern.

- If you score three on both factors, then again chose either sustainability or people.

- If you score below three on both, then dig deeper toward either the sustainability or people root.

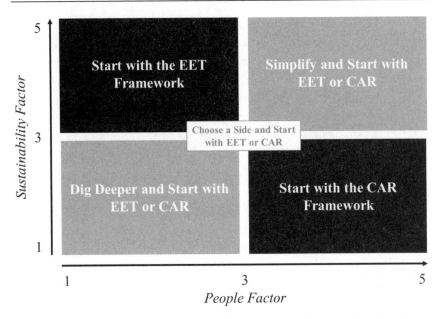

Figure 7.2 **The CLS Priority Matrix for connecting surface-level priorities with their systemic roots.**

Growing the Tree with Systemic Thinking and Enlightened Attention

Once you have your systemic starting point, you can then use the corresponding framework to initiate change—that is, CAR for people priorities, EET for sustainability priorities.

The CAR Framework: Competence, Autonomy, and Relatedness

If high-level people priorities such as talent retention and DEI are a primary concern, then the CAR framework can expose the interconnected roots overlooked in a specialized world. The framework delivers a next-level platform for specialists in areas such as talent management, engagement, and DEI to collaborate more effectively on these high-level people priorities.

Simply ask these specialists the following question: "What can we do to collectively increase the competence, autonomy, and relatedness of everyone—from job applicants to employees to customers and suppliers?" By making it about CAR-driven needs, you provide a cross-functional language to share jargon-free ideas. It moves your people away from concentrating on their own branches (and possibly reinventing wheels in siloes). Instead, it gets them focusing on the interconnected roots, as well as growing the whole tree of your organization. Getting to this root is an effective way to address all your people priorities in a single action. It's next-level leadership at its finest!

The EET Framework: The Exploration-Exploitation Trade-off

If surface-level sustainability priorities such as environmental concerns, product development, or acquisitions are your main leadership challenges, then the EET framework will help you think about the costs and benefits of exploiting old certainties versus exploring new possibilities.

Sustainability is a tension among ecological, economic, and social bottom lines, and EET will help you map the complex system of trade-offs necessary for achieving balance. EET's logic for (a) decreasing the exploitation of unsustainable old ways of doing, and (b) increasing the exploration of sustainable alternatives can be used to avoid crisis, increase preparedness and resilience, and calibrate sustainable growth. Various stakeholders can connect to co-create strategies for taming the tendency to overexploit (everything) while ensuring a smooth transition to a sustainable future. You might ask diverse specialists, "How can we sustainably exploit current ways of doing while exploring new opportunities throughout our organizational network?"

The Tony's Chocolonely story in Chapter 4 is a great example of a company growing success with this collective question. It regularly asks itself, its buyers, and its suppliers—as well as the consultancies and tech companies it hires—how it can exploit its deep knowledge for making and selling great chocolate while continually exploring opportunities for full transparency and sustainability, from bean to bar. Through this collective framework, the company is able to raise the (chocolate) bar on how to deliver ecological, economic, and social value.

The VUCA Common Denominator: Volatile, Uncertain, Complex, and Ambiguous

Finally, regardless of CAR or EET priorities, next-level leaders always have to account for a world that is perpetually VUCA. Volatility represents the speed and chaotic nature of change; uncertainty captures the reduced predictability in your environment; complexity stems from the interdependences, nonlinearities, and counterintuitive pathways embedded in hyper-connected, global systems; and ambiguity is the fog of decision-making resulting from both the known unknowns and the dreaded unknown unknowns. VUCA, simply put, is a common denominator.[24]

A good example is COVID-19. It's a rapidly changing event (*volatility*) blurring the outcome clarity of everything from mental health to supply chains (*uncertainty*). Pandemic recovery is also weakened due to its interconnectedness with other critical events such as the war in Ukraine (*complexity*), and it's playing out in an environment where there are many inevitable—though unknown—crises on the horizon (*ambiguity*).

Collectively, CAR, EET, and VUCA connect to most—if not all—of the surface-level priorities in your organization. They are fundamental challenges that will unlock many opportunities. The key is knowing what these roots need in order to thrive.

PAIRING SYSTEMIC NEEDS WITH DIGITAL TRENDS

Now that you've identified the underlying systemic root of your surface-level priority, it's time to develop a tailored set of growing instructions for your specific tree. For example, because VUCA is a common denominator, I know I'm always working in an inherently turbulent environment. So the first thing to do is understand (a) what the unique VUCA requirements are for each situation, and (b) how to turn those requirements into custom plans for change.

To address VUCA, I've identified the following requirements:

- VOLATILITY requires *sharing* for rapid adaptation.
- UNCERTAINTY requires *clarity* for increased confidence.

- COMPLEXITY requires *intelligence* for better predictability.

- AMBIGUITY requires *familiarity* for improved understanding.

I use these requirements to guide my selection of digital tools. For example, let's consider staffing challenges. Recruiting in a volatile labor market requires "matching tech" to quickly and accurately *share* data to identify talented individuals and pair them with open roles. Then, in addition to finding talent, innovations such as explainable AI will help *clarify* which employees to invest in for the greatest returns.[25,26,27]

Hyper-competitive (global) labor markets also increase situational complexity. This will drive the adoption of collective *intelligence* platforms—where AI can identify patterns in employment history, work habits, and many other factors, and then humans can transform this information into fresh insights for spotting hidden talent. Finally, the ramping up of ambiguity in business and society requires increasingly sophisticated predictive analytics. Predictive analytics allow organizations to more accurately anticipate shifts in workplace factors, including staffing needs and turnover. In other words, predictive analytics makes the future *familiar* and manageable.[28,29,30,31]

Broadly speaking, when it comes to VUCA you'll always need innovative ways to share data in order to remain competitive. You'll also need ever-improving ways to clarify and explain data, as well as platforms for leveraging the collective intelligence of human-machine interactions and tools for making the future familiar. Again, the goal is (a) to identify how VUCA is uniquely affecting your organization, and then (b) to adopt data and tech to meet the requirements of your situation.

In addition to VUCA (which is a part of every set of growing instructions), you can now start adding either CAR or EET needs to the checklist depending on where your priority falls on the CLS Priority Matrix.

For the CAR-related people priorities:

- COMPETENCE requires *access* to the benefits of an expanding global knowledge base.

- AUTONOMY requires *choice* to take advantage of increasingly flexible ways of living and working.

- RELATEDNESS requires *connectedness* to map, navigate, and engage vast networks of human and social capital.

For example, consider the employer concern about remote working and productivity. Some employers might be inclined to implement monitoring systems—but doing so can both demotivate employees and erode their trust in their employer. Instead, employees would benefit from advancements in knowledge-sharing systems that provide *access* to real-time answers from anyone and anywhere in the organization. In the future, every employee—from the CEO down—could have their "digital human" AI assistant find answers in policy documents, schedule appointments with colleagues, engage with someone else's digital human on a project, and more. No matter where or when, employees using these digital humans can make better *choices* because their AI-powered assistant uncovers insights hidden in a complex web of human, social, and organizational capital. Finally, improvements in mapping, navigating, and engaging the whole of an organization's human and social capital network will take the power of *connectivity* and community-building to the next level.[32,33,34]

Here, digital trends related to people priorities—regardless of context—will follow three clear trendlines that CLS-driven leaders can proactively leverage to motivate and engage others. First, contributing to and accessing an ever-expanding knowledge base will drive the development of smart systems for accurately recording and efficiently sharing know-how throughout an organization. Second, the evolution of successful technology will continue to provide stakeholders with the freedom of choice, such as how and when employees work, or mass individualized customization of consumer goods. Third, as the way we work and live changes, technology for turning virtual environments into fruitful spaces for nurturing connectivity and growth will flourish. Finding ways to use these trends in your context will help you increase stakeholder competence, autonomy, and relatedness. It will also improve trust, commitment, and other people factors indicative of great leadership.

For the EET-related sustainability priorities:

- EXPLOITATION requires *experience* to realize when old certainties are coming to an end.

- EXPLORATION requires *energy* to go beyond the horizon of short-term wins in order to achieve future discovery.

- TRADE-OFFS require *balance* between exploitation and exploration.

In the context of risk and financial governance, for example, functional leaders need to exploit their existing, siloed knowledge to protect their own patch of land. However, there is also a growing need to explore new approaches for defending against the cross-functional risks of the 21st century. To find a balance, decision-makers can surface and connect deep, siloed *experience* with solutions such as a "data fabric" to create an integrated, organization-wide source of truth. CLS-driven leaders who put their *energy* into exploring these solutions will thrive in a VUCA world—while their siloed counterparts work to merely survive. This shift to "dynamic risk governance," as Gartner puts it, "is statistically proven to drive high-quality risk behaviors, such as leadership striking the right *balance* of opportunities and business managers having the knowledge to make more risk-informed decisions."[35,36]

From a general perspective, challenges related to sustainability—such as environmental concerns and financial issues—require technology where CLS-driven leaders can find and use all the possible resources they have at their disposal to remain competitive in the short term while also investing in emerging technology that allows them to secure a long-term advantage. CLS-driven leaders who can leverage these technological trends for exploiting old certainties and exploring new possibilities will set the standard for 21st-century leadership.

The big takeaway is making sure you surround yourself with people who have the clarity and courage to see the need for change as well as the ability to express it. These teams are your guiding force for addressing VUCA environments, delivering CAR-driven needs, and balancing EET challenges. It's all about assembling the most effective team possible and co-creating solutions for next-level performance.

BUILDING CLS TEAMS

Society's urgent need for change requires CLS teams that can get at the systemic source of visible challenges. The script is no longer about a knight in shining armor heroically defeating a dragon. Rather, 21st-century challenges and opportunities require collaborative efforts to nurture the roots of an organization. We must move away from a Leviathan-like metaphor of a single "sovereign" and toward a tree-of-life view of organizational well-being where authority is distributed across diverse teams to foster growth.

It's your responsibility to establish these distinct but overlapping teams—one focused primarily on people factors and the other focused on sustainability—if you want to ensure the long-term viability of your organization. They will help you accomplish this mission-critical task by combining the breadth of cross-functional problem-solving with the depth of domain-expert knowledge.

In the next chapter, I'll elaborate on how to engage these CLS teams for game-changing transformation and sustainable growth. I'll highlight the value of installing a leadership process running on a collective, distributed, and shared system. I'll also share how you can make sure everyone in your team of systemic problem-solvers has a fair and equitable chance to provide input. This is your opportunity to ascend the heights of leadership by connecting relevant people, distributing relevant tasks, and sustaining necessary levels of motivation. It's your transformative journey to post-digital success, and together we'll navigate "the 4 Cs of post-digital co-creation."

CHAPTER 8

Navigating the 4 Cs of Digital Transformation

W elcome to the beginning of your transformative journey. You are about to set sail toward a land of great opportunity. Along the way you will develop co-creation practices combining the power of diversity with computational methods for turning concepts into action. And though the voyage at times will be challenging, or even tedious, the outcome will make you a fundamentally improved leader.

Before we begin, please note that this chapter is more of a step-by-step manual for digital transformation rather than a pithy commentary on the value of collaborative change. If you prefer some lighter reading for now, feel free to skip ahead to the concluding chapter, where I sum up everything and connect it all to Spider-Man.

MAKING (SYSTEMIC) GOALS CONCRETE AND ACTIONABLE

All aboard! It's time to explore the 4 Cs and co-create next-level change. This is where you, in collaboration with your core CLS teams, set up a workflow for achieving high-level goals. Adopted loosely from a standard machine-learning pipeline, my 4 Cs to post-digital co-creation are:

1. **Confirm** high-level priorities and the associated systemic frameworks.

2. **Collect** relevant cross-functional data and ideas to explore systemic challenges.

3. **Construct** cross-functional models for accomplishing high-level priorities.

4. **Convey** effective models in the form of policy and practice, monitor outcomes, and refine the process.

As discussed in the previous chapter, leaders wanting to build this sort of world-class CLS leadership process need to first focus on the deep, systemic issues related to people and sustainability—while always accounting for VUCA (volatility, uncertainty, complexity, and ambiguity). Exploring the underlying principles of systemic thinking allows you to see the connectedness of priorities and generate many visible solutions by achieving one systemic goal.

However, systemic problem-solving is not easy, and it unequivocally separates leaders from managers. Managers solve visible problems to keep business as usual, while leaders dive into systemic challenges—even if it is (economically) unpopular—in order to repair or replace the foundation. Leaders bring together diverse people—with potentially conflicting agendas—to collectively nurture the roots of business and society.

Co-Creating Next-Level Results

My 4 Cs are a practical guide for bringing these people together and driving lasting systemic change. They blend my academic work and applied experience with inspiration from two articles: a 2013 paper by Nambisan and Nambisan on engaging citizens in co-creation, and a 2019 publication by Nicholas and his colleagues on co-creation questions for effective research. The resulting framework spells out what teams need to do and the questions they need to ask in order to successfully navigate the 4 Cs of co-creation. Table 8.1 lays out each step, the leadership process at each stage, and the burning questions for change. Have a quick look to get an idea of what the 4 Cs are all about—though don't spend too much time on them just yet. We'll drill down into each step in the coming sections.[1,2]

The 4 Cs can be applied to any issue where opportunities spring from de-siloed collaboration—from business growth to employee

Table 8.1   CLS co-creation steps, co-creation leadership types, and questions for co-creating value.

Co-creation Steps	Co-creation Leadership Types	Co-creation Questions
Step 1 **Confirm** high-level priorities of interest and the underlying systemic root—e.g., ESG priorities connected to a sustainability root	**Expedition Leadership** Identifying, discovering, and defining high-level priorities and deep systemic-level challenges	• Based on the CLS Priority Matrix, is your priority a people challenge or a sustainability challenge? • Who needs to be involved in order to ensure we have a diverse understanding of the priority and its systemic root? • What co-creation tools will be necessary to help us transition from divergent thinking to convergent thinking?
Step 2 **Collect** relevant cross-functional data and ideas to explore systemic challenges	**Ideation Leadership** Conceptualizing actionable insights	• How do diverse perspectives see the underlying challenge? • What is the convergent goal? • Who benefits and how? • What are some quick wins?

(Continued)

Table 8.1   (Continued)

Co-creation Steps	Co-creation Leadership Types	Co-creation Questions
Step 3 **Construct** cross-functional models for accomplishing high-level priorities	**Simulation Leadership** Designing and developing actionable insights	• What does the initial prototype look like? • Who focuses on the nuts and bolts of development? • What are the ethical and legal ramifications?
Step 4 **Convey** effective models in the form of policy and practice, monitor outcomes, and refine the process	**Realization Leadership** Implementing actionable insights	• What does implementation look like? • Who focuses on implementation and impact? • How are follow-up adjustments handled?

well-being. And the 4 Cs enable CLS teams to make nimble shifts from one priority to the next. Teams can enhance people-oriented priorities, such as building a culture of empathy—and then rapidly switch their focus to balancing ESG outcomes and other sustainability-oriented goals.

If you want to be a leader making this sort of impact in an increasingly complex world, then CLS must become part of your daily leadership practice. You need to constantly ask, "How can CLS inform this decision, and how can I engage my CLS team to drive change?" Your transformation requires vision, motivation, and diligence to make CLS-driven leadership a habit.

For the remainder of this chapter, I'm going to elaborate on how each of the 4 Cs can augment both your vision and your motivation. It'll then be up to you—working with a CLS advisor—to become an ultramodern leader. Essentially, I'm buying you a gym membership, suggesting you get a personal trainer, and trusting you have the drive to make lasting change!

THE CONFIRM STEP

Purpose

This is a team-driven divergent thinking process to ensure you are nurturing the appropriate systemic roots of your high-level priorities. You bring together both sustainability- and people-oriented team members—from IT and finance leads to engagement and DEI specialists—for cross-fertilization and refinement of the CLS Priority Matrix task introduced in the previous chapter. It's the starting point of your collective journey.

Why This Step Is Important

The Confirm Step ensures the accurate selection of priorities in a never-ending and bewildering sea of data. It's an important step because choosing the wrong path is all too common. McKinsey, for example, found that "72% of senior executive respondents . . . said they thought bad decisions either were about as frequent as good ones or were the prevailing norm in their organization." This is why divergent thinking using diverse perspectives matters. It helps you avoid biases such as the confirmation bias—which is the tendency to search for, interpret, and act upon information confirming one's prior beliefs and values.[3,4]

To flesh this out more, I provide two case study examples:

CONSUMER NEEDS: Let's say the leadership of a company decides to prioritize service delivery—which is a classic people-oriented challenge—to address consumer needs. Indeed, a 2022 publication investigating the construction sector found that leaders frequently prioritize refining service delivery for customers over objectives such as making sustainable shifts in operations. They do this because their past experience confirms this service-oriented (and cost-effective) decision. And yet, it's also true that consumers in diverse sectors—including construction, energy/utilities, financial services, retail, and travel/

tourism—are adjusting their purchasing preferences. For example, in the sustainability chapter (Chapter 4) I highlight a 2021 study of over 10,000 consumers across 17 countries where 85% of respondents shifted to greener alternatives between 2016 and 2021. This significant change in behavior points to a need for leaders to address systemic challenges related to sustainability, not just service delivery. However, if leadership has a confirmation bias regarding staying the course versus changing tack, then that bias limits its ability to see the underlying systemic shift in the market, which could greatly affect the company's bottom line.[5,6]

This is where diverse CLS teams can help leaders realize that greener operations—a sustainability-oriented priority—might be the primary concern of their customers, more so than the current state of service delivery. CLS teams in this scenario would be reluctant to invest in unnecessary, people-oriented changes—such as alterations to service delivery—and would instead favor tending to the sustainability needs of their customers by going green.

REMOTE WORKING AND PRODUCTIVITY: Employees the world over are transitioning to remote working situations, and this has the potential to significantly boost productivity if leaders can effectively motivate their people. For example, a Catalyst survey of almost 7,500 employees across the globe found that key indicators of productivity—including creativity, engagement, and commitment—are all significantly higher when people have access to remote work options. Unfortunately, instead of nurturing employee autonomy, some leaders are inclined to focus on control—by tracking activity rather than impact—using invasive tools such as continuous video monitoring. They take these drastic, authoritarian steps because it confirms traditional beliefs on how to sustain productivity.[7]

However, this biased focus on sustaining productivity through control overlooks the people-oriented priority associated with a remote workforce. For example, applied research emerging since the pandemic clearly indicates that continuous monitoring reduces organizational citizenship behavior, trust, and performance—while increasing rates of burnout and turnover. These systems are starting to be seen as unethical "home invasions" that, ironically, hurt productivity.[8]

Here again, effective and diverse CLS teams can help leaders see that the real systemic root of productivity isn't a dehumanizing approach to sustaining control. Rather, next-level performance is rooted in universal people-oriented needs for supportive communities based on empathy and trust.

Getting down to the people or sustainability root of your priority is important because it helps you leverage previously unseen drivers of change. Like with any other problem-solving task, you have to first fully understand your challenge so you can make an effective plan, and then effectively carry out that plan. Getting this step wrong will have negative consequences throughout the co-creation process. Getting this step right will provide you with a strong foundation for transformation and growth.

The Takeaway

Make sure you bring together diverse individuals to assess your priority of interest so you can overcome the inevitable blind spots that stem from cognitive biases and siloes. The feedback from the collective wide-ranging thinking of CLS teams will help you correctly identify the root of your objectives—that is, people or sustainability roots—so you can work on making a broad systemic impact. This is an important starting point on your journey to next-level results.

The Necessary Leadership Process

Of course, it can be difficult to get several people to commit to a jointly convenient meeting time, let alone to facilitate effective group discussion and collaboration. And once the group is talking, you need to extract from a nebula of ideas distinct actionable insights with clear objectives. That's a monumental task; fortunately, it's one that leadership is perfectly suited to handle. You just have to know which process is necessary.

The Confirm Step requires what I call "expedition leadership": a leadership process that is adept at identifying, discovering, and defining high-level priorities and systemic frameworks. In the pantheon of leadership styles, expedition leadership aligns with a relationship-oriented style focused on team member well-being and satisfaction. Since there's likely to be conflict with diverse teams, it's essential to nurture and enable happy and healthy work relationships.

An expedition style also incorporates distributed leadership—where decision-making is spread across the CLS teams. It's important that all team members take a turn at leading through the Confirm Step since this is the best way to minimize bias, calibrate high-level priorities, and select the appropriate systemic framework to initiate the next steps.

Finally, it's up to you and your CLS advisor to establish and support the expedition leadership process. Effective leaders are great at conflict resolution and building high-performing teams—while CLS advisors are masters at selecting the right tools to support co-creation. Once you build this process, you can then set the co-creation wheels in motion with the following points for discussion.

Points for Discussion

I developed several prompts to guide team members in their exploration of the 4 Cs. They are a map, taking CLS teams from a well-defined priority to actionable insights for lasting change.

The prompts in the Confirm Step are designed to elicit divergent thinking regarding both (a) where you really *need* to go—remember, needs and wants are not the same thing—and (b) the necessary resources you need to overcome biased decision-making. Since the point of working with CLS teams is to connect the priorities at the branches of your organization with their systemic roots, you'll want to identify all potential points of connection in order to realize (many) surface-level opportunities—ideally within one unified mission. The following questions can help you find this focal point for change.

1. Based on the CLS Priority Matrix, is your priority a people challenge or a sustainability challenge?

Ask diverse team members—from HR directors to IT managers—to score your priority using the CLS Priority Matrix introduced in

Chapter 7. You'll want to encourage as much divergent thinking as possible about the people and sustainability factors of the Matrix. This diverse perspective will help you surface the hidden levers of change that often go unnoticed in a siloed world.

Consider the following example. The systemic root of growth perennially ranks first on Gartner's list of CEO priorities. As such, CEOs, CFOs, economists, and accountants, given their drive for economic performance, might give this priority a higher (financial) sustainability score using the matrix. Similarly, supply chain managers and IT leads, given their need for stable and secure operations, might also assign growth a higher sustainability score. On the other hand, HR directors, leadership development specialists, and organizational psychologists might look at growth from an employee performance perspective and accordingly score it more as a people challenge.[9]

Leaders receiving and duly considering this divergent input sets the stage for the concept of growth getting a debiased definition—which would subsequently influence how growth strategies evolve from there. For example, in the Tony's Chocolonely case from Chapter 4, the company's definition of growth is people oriented, and all its practices reflect this commitment to collective well-being—from ensuring exceptional pay for their farmers to ensuring steady gains for their investors.

Tip: You can have team members complete the CLS Priority Matrix separately and then compare scores to get the discussion started. This is a quick and easy way to get standardized feedback.

2. Who needs to be involved in order to ensure we have a diverse understanding of the priority and its systemic root?

This next step is to ensure that the appropriate domain experts and cross-functional leads are enlisted to address the systemic challenge. If your priority gets a higher sustainability score using the matrix, then the composition of the CLS team needs to match the task. For example, addressing the need for green supply chains will call for enlisting the internal managers who oversee logistics, finance, IT, and procurement. Additional external domain experts might include ecologists, environmental economists, and any other practitioner or scholar specializing in supply chains.

But if your priority gets a higher people-oriented score—such as employee engagement and motivation—then the internal leaders to enlist would be the DEI leads, directors of employee experience, sales and marketing managers, and workforce analytics specialists. In this case, ideal external input could be solicited from behavioral economists, social psychologists, and other experts with deep knowledge in human behavior.

Also, note that focusing on a people-oriented root or a sustainability-oriented root does *not* exclude expertise from the other side. Working with the 4 Cs is not an either-or process. People and sustainability factors overlap. For instance, even if you identify growth as a people-oriented challenge, specialists in finance, IT, and logistics still have a major role to play: they're essential for building the infrastructure and taking the practical steps necessary for realizing people-oriented solutions. Similarly, if the priority is rooted in sustainability, such as green supply chains, then support from the people side is necessary both to encourage buy-in of greener operations and to motivate sustainable change.

The main goal is to incorporate as many relevant stakeholders as possible. Like in the meta-leadership framework discussed in the crisis chapter, leaders need to bring together diverse and relevant superiors, colleagues, subordinates, and external stakeholders. This is because you're building a cross-functional team tailored to the root of your priority, whether it's people oriented or sustainability oriented.

> *Tip: Your CLS advisor will be a key player at this stage, so be sure to select an advisor with broad, de-siloed knowledge—and rely on that advisor heavily.*

3. What co-creation tools will be necessary to help us transition from divergent thinking to convergent thinking?

There are a wide range of co-creation tools—from digital tools allowing for scalable, asynchronous co-creation to in-person sticky-note mind-mapping in order to connect diverse keywords to a central concept. Work with your advisor to choose tools based on your time and geographic constraints. If everyone is local and available, then go with in-person tools. If your group cannot *all* meet in person, then select a tool with time and geographic flexibility—especially if the team is spread across time zones. My personal recommendation is a hybrid approach: start with a digital mind-mapping tool for everyone to provide asynchronous individual input, and then arrange an in-person or video conference meeting to collectively decide upon the priority and the systemic root. (Note, if most of your group can meet in person with even just one exception, I urge you to *not* hold a discussion meeting with an uneven playing field, so to speak. If one person could only attend via video, then everyone should attend via video. This detail is essential to effective diversity!)

> *Tip: On the day of the team meeting, have everyone first share their ideas paired one-on-one using a "speed dating" session. They each take turns explaining what they think the high-level priority and associated systemic root is, and then they spend two minutes discussing the similarities and differences in their thinking. You can do this in person or in virtual breakout rooms using video conferencing software. This simple communication approach can save a lot of time and resolve a lot of conflict in advance, making your meeting that much more productive.*

THE COLLECT STEP

Purpose

Once the priority's starting point has been confirmed as either a people-oriented or a sustainability-oriented challenge, the respective CLS team takes the lead. The purpose of the Collect Step is to work with these cross-functional leaders and domain experts to conceptualize actionable insights. This step is about initiating the process from divergent thinking to convergent *doing*. In other words, it's time to discuss the details of how you're going to bring about change.

Why This Step Is Important

The Collect Step ensures divergent ideas and data are uniformly channeled into decision-making. This requires a mosaic of people with diverse KSAOs—knowledge, skills, abilities, and other characteristics—identifying and sharing insights. When you implement an effective platform for connecting and engaging these individuals, you will produce game-changing insights. For example, a large Deloitte survey of over 1,000 leaders found that 80% of executives surveyed exceeded their business goals by using—across their enterprise—a single, common set of tools and methods for accessing and analyzing data. These organizations are not reinventing wheels in silos. Instead, they're establishing a systemic approach to work on the collective mission. Just as in rugby, everyone's working together makes for an effective push.[10]

An example of this unified push is "Tony's Beantracker." This is part of the chocolates company's best-in-class supply chain for collective and sustainable growth. The platform is a transparent space where everyone involved in its supply chain—from growers to exporters to their manufacturers—is connected for full traceability from "bean to bar." This ensures a diverse and complex network is working as one to accomplish its mission to make 100% slave-free chocolate.[11]

The Collect Step, as Tony's Chocolonely epitomizes, is where issues are always surfaced and every CLS team member has an equal opportunity to address conflicts of interest, solve problems, and add value. Depending on the size and geographic spread of the CLS team, platforms for collecting ideas can range from a series of in-person roundtable discussions to videoconferencing to virtual workplaces to virtual reality offices if you want to get immersive and fancy.[12]

The Takeaway

Make sure you provide a platform for turning divergent individuals into convergent teams. In other words, nurture teams that can increase organizational performance through high levels of engagement, cooperative norms, and trust. It's in this diverse, equitable, and inclusive space where great ideas emerge.[13]

The Necessary Leadership Process

The big leadership challenge in Step 2 (Collect) is building an eco-system to collect and transform divergent ideas into convergent action. It's all about nurturing joint ideation through compromise and the reduction of personal agendas for the good of the team. Without this collaborative ecosystem, individuals won't operate as teams. Instead, people will often work to defend territory and compete for limited resources. Fortunately, leadership is a fantastic adaptation for building and maintaining high-performing communities with varied backgrounds.[14]

Leadership encourages individuals to rise above self-interest and see the need for collective change. It also has the ability to provide a clear, inspirational, and de-siloed vision of the future. Going further, modern leadership also has the ability to fully leverage the power of DEI-infused convergent input. As the Center for Creative Leadership notes, those with network perspectives "identify patterns of relationships and people in their personal network and the broader organizational network that will foster strategic success." Leadership incorporating this network perspective quickly identifies people who are being marginalized and removes barriers to engagement.[15]

I'm calling this ability to encourage collective change, establish de-siloed vision, and promote DEI-driven engagement "ideation leadership"—a style relating closely to transformational leadership with a distinct focus on diverse, equitable, and inclusive transitioning from divergent thinking to convergent doing.

Points for Discussion

The four prompts for the Collect Step are specifically designed to promote this transition to doing. You explored as many perspectives as possible in the first step—with a mix of people-oriented and sustainability-oriented team members ranging from DEI experts to financial leads. This divergent process allows you to accurately identify the systemic root of your priority. In the Collect Step, diverse ideas converge, and you're able to tend to the systemic roots of your high-level priorities using the following questions.

1. How do diverse perspectives see the underlying challenge?

This is where you start fleshing out solutions with a common language based on the CAR or EET framework defined in Chapter 7. For example, if a data scientist wants to share results regarding employee engagement (a people factor) with someone who has no background in data and statistics, then that data scientist would ideally speak in terms of *competence, autonomy, and relatedness* to establish a common ground. Relatedly, if an ESG expert wants to talk with someone who has no experience with balancing economic and environmental outcomes, then that ESG expert should discuss the dilemma in terms of *exploiting* old certainties versus *exploring* new opportunities. Not everybody will know the finer points of ESG or data science, but they will understand the basic concepts of CAR and EET. This approach allows more people to connect, converge, and co-create next-level opportunities for growth.

Establishing this common ground minimizes the haze of jargon and enables the free flow of collective ideas. For instance, recall the Porsche example in Chapter 4: the car manufacturer works with internal and external parties to develop innovative solutions for eliminating costly interruptions to production while also "reducing the environmental impact across the whole value chain." They created a digital twin platform where diverse perspectives can converge and collectively test trade-offs between *exploitation* and *exploration*. It's a virtual space where team members can focus on systemic challenges with a universal language.[16]

> Tip: When opposing views emerge, have your team do a SWOT— strength, weaknesses, opportunities, and threats—analysis or some other strategic planning process. This approach allows you to surface barriers to co-creation in a very organized way.

2. What is the convergent goal?

It's time to have your CLS team identify specific goals to further crystalize diverse, divergent thinking into convergent doing. The logic is moving people toward collective action. To help them along, you may want to use a SMART framework.

SMART goals—as directly quoted in the original article—should be:

Specific—target a specific area for improvement;

Measurable—quantify or a least suggest an indicator of progress;

Assignable—specify who will do what;

Realistic—state what results can realistically be achieved given available resources; and

Time-related—specify when the result(s) can be achieved.[17]

Let's consider how SMART goals relate to a hypothetical where you're leading a team to address customer demands for greener supply chains.

Have your team collectively decide on a **specific** area for improvement. They may want to *explore* supply-chain decarbonization. Next, they need to locate **measurable** indicators of decarbonization somewhere along the supply chain. (As an example, BMW announced it is requiring all suppliers of high-voltage batteries to include their carbon emissions as part of the tendering process. This is an important, quantifiable step that will help the carmaker lower its overall emissions per vehicle—perhaps by as much as 80%.[18]) For the **assignable** task, have everyone identify how they can contribute to the decarbonization goal based on their expertise. So, for example, marketing and communications will work on framing this decarbonization goal for customers, supply chain analysts can explore decarbonization best-practices, CFOs will crunch the numbers, and so on.

Next, make sure the goal is **realistic**. You don't need a room full of finance and accounting types overemphasizing the short-term costs of decarbonizing. This is about letting your diverse CLS team find a realistic balance between costs and benefits. Finally, set a **time-related** deadline. This is a must when working with cross-functional teams that are likely consumed with individual demands in their silos.

Tip: Make sure your team knows that these goals are not commitments at this stage. They're temporary guideposts on your journey

to convergent doing. Also, this task is not a huge time commitment. It's an in-person chat or video conference that you and your advisor can refine into a collective SMART goal.

3. Who benefits and how?

This question is primarily about keeping each CLS team member motivated. Have everyone on the team articulate how they and their stakeholders will benefit from accomplishing the collective SMART goal. Benefits can include anything from meeting individual KPIs to addressing large social issues. Aligning these perceived benefits across your CLS team will help ensure cohesion for the duration of the journey.

Back to our sustainable supply chain example, the benefits for some will easily emerge while others might need some extra attention. If a supply chain–minded ecologist is on the team (and they should be), then they will easily see the benefits of robust decarbonization. Marketing and communications heads who are keenly aware of the customer need for sustainability will also find benefit in the goal. Where the challenge lies are with those who fear too drastic of a switch will negatively affect shareholder value and their ability to hit personal targets. This is where an effect ideation leader needs to emerge and inspire a shared vision.

For example, Larry Fink, CEO of BlackRock, writes an annual letter to his fellow CEOs on achieving long-term stability. In these letters he regularly emphasizes the value of sustainability and decarbonization. As he eloquently noted in a 2022 letter:

> Most stakeholders—from shareholders, to employees, to customers, to communities, and regulators—now expect companies to play a role in decarbonizing the global economy. Few things will impact capital allocation decisions—and thereby the long-term value of your company—more than how effectively you navigate the global energy transition in the years ahead.[19]

In other words, help CLS team members find their respective benefits and unite their individual needs into a collective action plan.

Tip: It's extremely important that everyone on the CLS team sees how this journey offers personalized value. This is not about catering to selfish impulses. Instead, satisfying diverse team-member needs at this stage spreads buy-in to a much larger audience—because they're connected to stakeholders with similar concerns. For instance, if a CFO and a consumer advocate feel good about the same sustainability goal, then they'll likely share that warm glow through their networks. This is how transformation takes hold.

4. What are some quick wins?

Now that a common language is established, SMART goals are set, and diverse interests are aligned, it's time to get some quick wins. You want to demonstrate how this co-creation process will produce rapid results through collective action. Generating answers to this question sets the stage for the next-level innovation you and your CLS team will construct in Step 3.

Tip: Really focus on the most attainable aspects of your SMART goal. Use this quick win approach so everyone stays motivated on the long term—where the real gold is waiting.

THE CONSTRUCT STEP

Purpose

The purpose of this step is to build a testable model of your initiative before deployment. Depending on the type and scope of your priority, models can range from relatively simple statistical representations of individual-level concerns such as the factors predicting high levels of work engagement in remote working situations to inter-organizational simulations of large-scale initiatives such as decarbonization of global supply chains. This is the stage where the computational experts really start to shine. They will help you and your CLS team anticipate any hidden obstacles on your journey and provide valuable course corrections.

Why This Step Is Important

You can experiment and stress-test your proposed initiative in a safe, transparent, and inclusive environment. Computational experimentation also reduces costs and increases the pace and quality of outcomes. McKinsey, for example, recently reported on an automotive OEM—original equipment manufacturer—using digital twin technology for early-phase development. As it explains:

> The start of the development process is especially challenging for complex products because the various stakeholder groups, such as sales, engineering, and finance, may have different or even contradictory product requirements. The OEM now balances these trade-offs using a digital concept configurator that allows for simultaneous evaluation of customer requirements, technical concepts, and product costs. When a technical concept within a system or subsystem of the product is changed, the implications for meeting customer requirements or product cost targets become immediately transparent.

McKinsey also goes on to note that this tech-enabled, cross-functional approach allowed the company to reduce material costs by 5–10%.[20]

The Takeaway

Computational tools for experimentation and development are rapidly becoming a must-have. They form a protective barrier—that is, a digital proving ground—between ideation and implementation. They also help diverse CLS teams see differing perspectives in a safe space, and they help leaders leverage the full power of joint decision-making using realistic, low-risk simulations.

The Necessary Leadership Process

The big leadership challenge in Step 1 was drumming up as much divergent thinking as possible to identify the systemic root of your priority. Then, in Step 2, you had to build a CLS team and ensure it thinks of convergent plans for doing. Now, the big challenge is bringing on board the necessary technical experts to help your CLS team build and test a model of its actionable insights.

The Construct Step requires a leadership process able to blend traditional leadership competencies (critical thinking, motivation, etc.) with technical competencies such as translating conceptual insights into concrete technical terms related to scope, build requirements, and constraints. Taking advantage of this powerful step also requires finding a balance between overbuilding and underbuilding models for testing initiatives. If leadership sacrifices too much resolution, then they'll build invalid models, which can encourage the implementation of false and harmful ideas. On the other hand, insisting on a hyper-realistic model can lead to unnecessary spending and time investment when something much simpler (and less expensive) would do.

The leadership process for blending traditional leadership and technical competencies and finding this important balance in model construction is what I'm calling "simulation leadership." As a simulation leader, you have to make sure the CLS team doesn't devolve into technical versus non-technical expertise. This is where traditional leadership competencies related to team cohesion come into play. Also, if you come from a non-technical background, then rely on your CLS advisor to help you understand the concerns of technical team members when it comes to translating conceptual insights into concrete technical output. Remember, simulation leadership is about blending expertise and building the right model—not too complicated, not too basic—for boosting performance through testing. Following are three critical points for finding this balance.

Points for Discussion

1. What does the initial prototype look like?

This is where your CLS team translates conceptual needs for goal attainment into concrete technical statements regarding the nuts and bolts of your model. It's the question where leadership threads the needle between over- and underbuilding a model to reach its goal.

Tip: Use your traditional leadership competencies such as emotional intelligence to assess both the technical and non-technical members of your CLS team. If divisions are forming and one side feels unhappy and unheard, then the prototype is likely unbalanced—that is, it's either being overbuilt and the model is complicated (which upsets the technical experts) or it's being underbuilt and the model doesn't accurately capture reality (which upsets the non-technical team members). Put simply, leaders can oversee many aspects of a technical build even if they lack the background. It's more about people dynamics and finding balance than tech skills.

2. Who focuses on the nuts and bolts of development?

The technical members of your team will primarily focus on the nuts and bolts. These team members will also need to recruit internal and external technical support based on the specific requirement of the prototype. For example, building a digital twin environment to simulate sustainable supply chain trade-offs requires different expertise relative to a smart platform able to customize leadership training based on individual needs.

Tip: Don't just shift this question to the technical members of your team. Such a shift runs the risk of prioritizing technical capability over conceptual needs. You must ensure the technical specialist focusing on development maintain balance with the conceptual requirements of your non-technical team members. Interpersonal communication skills such as clarity and frequency of message are a must.

3. What are the ethical and legal ramifications?

A thorough summary of this question requires its own book. Instead, here's the abridged version:

Privacy and transparency have to be baked into every prototype from the start. Your team has several considerations to address from the outset such as how data is going to be handled, how you will introduce "explainable AI" into the build to identify and remove bias, what is an appropriate balance between privacy and transparency, and what are the legal factors informing the build.

> *Tip: Work with your CLS advisor to identify relevant data compli-
> ance and protection experts, data ethicists, explainable AI specialists,
> and so on. They are the people you need to operate ethically and legally
> in the present environment, and they will help you proactively adjust
> to future changes in privacy law and ethical expectations.*

THE CONVEY STEP

Purpose

Once the prototype is constructed and tested (in small pockets of the intended audience), it's now time to broadly convey the CLS-driven initiative. The scope and number of people involved to accomplish this task depends on the priority. Decarbonizing a global supply chain, for example, is a much more complex deployment than focusing on employee engagement in a small enterprise. In other words, the purpose of this step is figuring out who needs to be involved with implementation, where they need to be involved, for how long, and what resources are necessary to scale up from a test environment to production.

Why This Step Is Important

This step is critical for ensuring all the hard work and resources used to get this far along don't go to waste. Gartner, for instance, forecasted IT spending to reach $4.4 trillion in 2022. Unfortunately, a Deloitte survey in June 2022 found that fewer than half of the 551 executive and board members they surveyed "believe their board is providing enough oversight to technology matters." They cited the following top five challenges to effective oversight:

1. Overreliance on management for decision-making;

2. Deficits in tech fluency on the board;

3. Unclear governance structure around technology concerns;

4. Management information on tech matters is not well-defined; and

5. The links between technology and strategy are unclear.

The same survey also found that "fewer than half of the respondents feel good about their organization's tech leadership." So organizations are spending astronomical amounts of money on digital strategic initiatives while having little confidence regarding the necessary support for success. This is a "make it or break it" moment where you can truly become a next-level, CLS-driven leader.[21,22]

The Takeaway

The Convey Step gets you and your CLS team across the line. It's easy to lose steam at the end. A strong push past the finish is absolutely necessary. There's a lot at stake, requiring buy-in from the board to the front line. Don't let up!

The Necessary Leadership Process

The big leadership challenge is leading on all fronts. You are taking a model developed by a relatively small CLS team and putting it out into a much larger organizational world. This is a fragile time where board members can fail to see the connection between your output and their strategic priorities, managers can push back to preserve their established practices, employees can struggle with learning new systems, and suppliers can become frustrated with changes to existing operations.

Given these various pitfalls, the Convey Step requires a leadership process with the ability to lead down the formal hierarchy, lead across to peers within and between silos, influence superiors above, and lead beyond by engaging with suppliers, collaborating organizations, customers, governmental agencies, and any other external stakeholder. This is what I'm calling "realization leadership." You are taking a carefully constructed model from the Construct Step and making it a reality in the Convey Step.

Realization leaders are all about meta-leadership—a process for providing guidance, direction, and momentum across organizational lines that then develops into a shared course of action and commonality among diverse stakeholders.

Creating a shared course of action and commonality requires transformational interactions with individuals across all organizational lines to inspire buy-in, and it also involves a pinch of transactional leadership to monitor implementation, reward adoption, and correct any problems with scaling up from prototype to reality. The following questions will help you attain this transformational cooperation and transactional supervision to realize the full potential of your initiative.

Points for Discussion

1. What does implementation look like?

This is an interesting question because implementation doesn't look the same for everyone. A board member will see the product of your sustainable supply chain initiative differently from a supply chain manager, for instance. Not considering this difference in perspective can have a devastating impact on implementation because each stakeholder's wants, needs, and pains are not fully understood.

> *Tip: To address this question, rely on the diversity of your team— its cross-functional, mosaic-like composition—to establish buy-in and lead implementation across organizational lines. The goal of this exercise is to anticipate the wants, needs, and pains of every stakeholder within this sphere of importance.*

2. Who focuses on implementation and impact?

Everyone on your CLS team is to some degree responsible for focusing on implementation and impact. Rely on this cross-functional team to monitor and address the barriers and drivers of implementation from multiple perspectives.

> *Tip: I can't stress enough the value of diversity in this step. Establishing a diverse perspective is arguably the number one priority for understanding implementation and impact. Ensure your*

team works like an organization-wide monitoring system that con-
tinually funnels feedback in from as many stakeholders as possible.
CLS-driven leaders actively work to create, maintain, and increase
these streams of information. It's these streams that turn into a river
of knowledge for game-changing transformation and growth.

3. How are follow-up adjustments handled?

Assign specific members of your team to oversee feedback from different organizational lines and stakeholder groups. Then hub these various streams of feedback into a collective understanding of how your
initiatives are progressing at four stations: at the top, at the front line,
across to peers, and with external stakeholders. Finally, take this 360°
view and use it both to inform further experimentation and to refine
your plans of action.

> *Tip: Use the data and tech I discussed in the previous chapters to*
> *establish a continuous flow of 360° feedback. Use pulse surveys,*
> *sentiment analysis, and whatever else you have access to for gain-*
> *ing insights. This input will help you adjust and improve your*
> *initiatives with increasing accuracy.*

CONCLUDING THOUGHTS

There's no doubt that navigating the 4 Cs requires a lot of effort and
potentially a significant investment of resources. However, taking an
intuitive approach or "passing this off to the techy people" is ultimately
far more time consuming and resource heavy—and much more likely
to fail. Instead, CLS-driven leaders are leaning into this post-digital
environment with purpose and direction. They're building diverse
teams, and they're hungry for new frameworks to drive change.

At the end of the day, society is experiencing a paradigm shift in
leadership, and you have an amazing opportunity to help make history.
You just have to refine your vision, stay focused, and make computational leadership your new habit. I wish you the best of luck on this
journey of discovery and growth.

CONCLUSION: SPIDER-MAN AND YOUR POST-DIGITAL FUTURE

I started this book with a story about impoverished leadership destroying my hometown. In closing, I'll share a more uplifting anecdote. On November 2, 1927, a man named Steve Ditko was born in my working-class neighborhood in Johnstown, Pennsylvania. Upon graduating in 1945, Steve enlisted in the US Army, where he drew comics for an Army newspaper while stationed in Allied-occupied Germany. Following his discharge, Steve moved to New York City and enrolled in art school to refine his craft. He worked intensively for two years sharpening his talents and eventually caught the attention of Stan Lee. The two developed a close working relationship and, in August 1962, something "amazing" happened: they co-created Spider-Man. I share this story because it always makes me think of the adage popularized by the Spider-Man comics: "In this world, with great power there must also come—great responsibility!"

You, as CLS-driven leaders, and the CLS-driven leadership processes you create, must display this essential mix of digital strength and maturity. The risks are too great if you don't establish such a balance. For example, digital strength (having all the resources you need) paired with digital immaturity (*not* knowing what solutions are needed) runs the risk of implementing toxic data and tech. The resulting outcomes could include catastrophic breaches of privacy, crippling costs, and the reinforcement of biased and discriminatory practices— very much like using a driver in a sand trap instead of the wedge in your bag. Conversely, having the maturity to know what solutions are necessary without having the resources creates the potential for being left behind. Subsequent costs to this scenario include decreased efficiency and productivity, reduced operational awareness, a higher chance of human error, and limited talent management. Sticking with the golf metaphor, it's knowing a wedge is necessary but not having one available.

161

Overcoming this imbalance is where CLS-driven leaders shine. Their superpower is attaining buy-in from the top down and knowing how to surround themselves with the necessary experts to wield this influence responsibly. Their superior blend of strength and maturity allows them to tackle most challenges and extract next-level benefits for their organization. These CLS-driven leaders are able to see beyond the horizon with data and tech, and raise the bar when it comes to factors such as engagement, preparedness, sustainability, and well-being. Simply put, they consistently select the right shot *and* the right club.

LEARNING FROM INTERCONNECTED KNOWLEDGE

To increase your strength and maturity, I shared insights with you from decision-makers at leading companies. Now, to wrap this up, I've highlighted six interconnected seeds of knowledge I extracted from these interviews:

FOCUS: At the core of every CLS-driven initiative is a clear set of goals directly connected to core business. Every participant stressed this point from the start of the interview. A good portion of time was first dedicated to setting the foundation, the *why* of their digital transformation. We then moved on to the *how* in terms of data and tech. This "why before how" approach is a clear step toward digital maturity. All interviewees know what digital clubs to use and when to use them.

VARIETY: The *how* portion of each interview included mention of the various streams of data and types of technology being utilized in that company's digital transformation. All of the organizations blend traditional and familiar tools, such as surveys, with more advanced alternatives, such as Tony's Chocolonely's Open Chain tools for precise monitoring of people and operations. This variety of data and tech—directly connected to their core business—highlights their digital strength. These leaders have an appropriately diverse set of clubs in their bag.

SUPPORT: All of the organizations rely on data scientists, engineers, behavioral scientists, and other subject-matter experts to effectively wrap their resources around core business goals. Whether internally sourced in large organizations such as IBM and Microsoft or outsourced in the case of Tony's, this network of support operates like a system of satellites monitoring challenges and providing insights. It's an interconnected web designed to increase digital strength and maturity through diverse expert perspectives.

BALANCE: The participants also expressed the need to balance immediate and incremental change with boundary-expanding experimentation and innovation. As a clear sign of their digital maturity, they understand that the height of crisis and disruption is not the time for radical change. Instead, the innovative push, in the form of organizational learning and adaption, needs to come proactively before the chaos or just following the turmoil. It's like taking lessons with a golf pro before playing, then playing a round with the pro watching, and finally debriefing with the pro to discuss performance and opportunities for improvement. Basically, it's a cyclical process of preparing, performing, learning, and improving.

COMMUNITY: Another common theme was community building among their end users. JPMorgan Chase, for example, is investigating CLS-driven ways to better connect diverse groups globally to increase inclusivity, and IBM is using CLS-driven leadership development to build a community of "IBMers" focused on transformation and growth. These organizations are rapidly improving their ability to link and leverage their human and social capital with data and tech.

LEADERSHIP: There was also an unequivocal emphasis on the need for buy-in from the very top of the organization. All of the digital maturity in the world amounts to nothing if there isn't direction, mandates, decision rights, ownership, and accountability. Such factors provide the strength necessary to get CLS-driven initiatives off the ground.

I can't stress enough how important buy-in from the top is for each interviewee. From my personal experience, there's nothing more frustrating and demotivating than having a game-changing plan ready to implement only to find out that, instead of receiving a healthy budget and talent, you get lip service and box ticking. At times, CLS-driven leaders will have to overcome this digital apathy using tactics such as introducing "the fear of missing out," making it clear CLS-driven approaches are the new standard, and using storytelling like my Henry Clay Frick example at the beginning of the book, which demonstrates the need to change and stay on the right side of history.[1]

Finally, it's interesting to note that all of the leaders I spoke with monitor these six interconnected components over time and at multiple levels. They do so to gain a deeper understanding of how, where, and when CLS-driven initiatives are affecting performance. By incorporating all six factors over time and space, they are creating a strong and mature ecosystem for ushering in post-digital excellence. Leaders on this path are, without a doubt, setting the new standard of leadership. And, in having read this book, you are part of this pioneering journey to new lands of opportunity.

Boldly Going Where No Leader Has Gone Before

It's important that you see this need for CLS-driven discovery because there's no going back to "normal." Decades of systemic unsustainability and the current wave of new technologies have forever changed the concept of normal. Society's lack of preparedness for COVID-19 and the devastating impact of climate change are just two examples of how unsustainability is altering business and society. Likewise, the democratization of tools such as machine learning and the open access to big data means that huge tech-driven disruption can come from anyone, anywhere, at any time. And, if that weren't enough, highly funded initiatives are emerging where senior executives from leading companies are collaborating with the brightest in science and tech to overwhelm and outpace their competition. JPMorgan Chase, for example, teamed up with IBM in pursuit of the "quantum advantage"—a stage when quantum computing exponentially increases a leader's decision-making capabilities. It's estimated that JP could make and save billions for their clients and shareholders before the competition is able to follow suit.[2]

The risk of inaction is why you need to go to the edge and beyond in terms of research and application. This doesn't mean you have to invest huge amounts of resources and learn how to program in Python. You can, however, dispatch a small taskforce of subject-matter experts, data scientists, and engineers for digital reconnaissance because they'll help you remain prepared, agile, and resilient, at minimal cost.

Let's briefly look at what such a CLS taskforce might find beyond the edge. First, related to the potential advantage of quantum-based decision-making are digital twin initiatives. Once the artificial twin is powered by a quantum engine, these "mirror worlds" will likely provide an amazingly precise and real-time bridge between the physical and digital worlds. Richard Feynman, a Nobel Prize winner in physics and the godfather of quantum computing, wrote: "Nature isn't classical, dammit, and if you want to make a simulation of nature, you'd better make it quantum mechanical [to handle the complexity]." This means that CLS-driven leaders of the future can theoretically model everyone and everything in their organization and simulate billions of complex scenarios to help them optimize everything from employee engagement at the individual level to supply chain management on a global scale. Indeed, scientists are starting to apply a quantum approach to predicting both human behavior and the likelihood of achieving strategic objectives.[3,4,5]

Second, AI may one day completely remove the mundane aspects of management from leadership. This is why you shouldn't be concerned about the machine replacing you. AI is not very good at creativity and vision—the domain of leaders. It is, however, great at finding complex patterns, performing routine tasks, and eliminating errors—the domain of management. Thus, counter to prevailing doom and gloom scenarios, AI will liberate leadership.

For example, AI-driven digital humans can help identify your routine tasks, automate them, and ultimately delete them from your life so you're free to be a productive leader. An AI assistant could continuously answer all of your emails and calls—day and night—and then alert you to the messages requiring your personal response. AI agents could also help you find tendering opportunities with a high probably of success and continually improve their performance based on previous outcomes—something referred to as "reinforcement learning." You might even find these AI assistants sitting next to you in immersive virtual meetings. In real time, they could record everything that's said and then produce draft reports and proposals with problem statements, solutions, budgets, and planning immediately ready for your revision. Again, it's all about removing the management tasks so you can be a next-level leader.[6]

A final example of life beyond the edge is the challenge of achieving universal Internet connectivity. Nearly 3 billion people—or 37% of the world's population—have never used the Internet. This is an amazing amount of untapped human and social capital that can help fuel the knowledge economy. By bringing these individuals into the digital fold, society and economies will experience a profound surge of innovation and growth. It's definitely something CLS-driven leaders should monitor, promote, and leverage, despite the existing barriers to worldwide connectivity. Like the quantum advantage, once a tipping point is reached, CLS-driven leaders will enjoy a "connectivity advantage."[7]

CONCLUDING THOUGHTS

The leaders of today and tomorrow have so many wonderful opportunities to set the stage for a bright future. You will likely experience more technological progress in the coming 10 years than what was experienced in the previous 100. That's why it's so important you both understand CLS-driven change and learn how to use it to shape the future. Possessing this superpower allows you to eat uncertainty for breakfast and see return on investments while others huddle in the corner wondering what happened.

Whether you're ready or not, business and society is entering a time of perpetual disruption. The catastrophic level of risk in this environment requires data, tech, and talent to unlock effective solutions. You must engage this nexus of knowledge in order to successfully lead your organization through the challenges ahead. You can no longer rely on the intuitive leadership styles of the past to address present and future needs—intuition simply won't cut it. So prepare yourself: the computational revolution has arrived!

NOTES

INTRODUCTION: HOW A FLOOD IN JOHNSTOWN, PENNSYLVANIA, INSPIRED COMPUTATIONAL LEADERSHIP

1. "The Dam Was Owned by the South Fork Fishing & Hunting Club," *Johnstown Area Heritage Association*, https://www.jaha.org/attractions/johnstown-flood-museum/flood-history/the-club-and-the-dam/.
2. David McCullough, *The Johnstown Flood* (New York: Simon & Schuster, 2007).
3. Brian R. Spisak, "How Data Can Make Better Managers," *Harvard Business Review*, March 2, 2022, https://hbr.org/2022/03/how-data-can-make-better-managers.
4. Brian R. Spisak, "Warriors and Peacekeepers: Testing a Biosocial Implicit Leadership Hypothesis of Intergroup Relations Using Masculine and Feminine Faces," *PLOS ONE* 7, no. 1 (2012): e30399, https://doi.org/10.1371/journal.pone.0030399.
5. Paulo C. Simões-Lopes, Marta E. Fabián, and João O. Menegheti, "Dolphin Interactions with the Mullet Artisanal Fishing on Southern Brazil: A Qualitative and Quantitative Approach," *Revista Brasileira de Zoologia* 15 (1998): 709–726, https://doi.org/10.1590/S0101-81751998000300016.
6. Gregory Ferenstein, "Netflix CEO Explains Why 'Gut' Decisions Still Rule in the Era of Big Data," *Forbes*, January 22, 2016, https://www.forbes.com/sites/gregoryferenstein/2016/01/22/netflix-ceo-explains-why-gut-decisions-still-rule-in-the-era-of-big-data/?sh=61893911e09c.

CHAPTER 1: DEVELOPING THE ROBERTO CLEMENTES OF LEADERSHIP

1. Michael Lewis, *Moneyball: The Art of Winning an Unfair Game* (New York: W. W. Norton, 2004).
2. "Size of the Training Industry," *Training Industry*, March 29, 2021, https://trainingindustry.com/wiki/learning-services-and-outsourcing/size-of-training-industry/.

3. David V. Day and Lisa Dragoni, "Leadership Development: An Outcome-Oriented Review Based on Time and Levels of Analyses," *Annual Review of Organizational Psychology and Organizational Behavior* 2, no. 1 (2015): 133–156.

4. Brian R. Spisak, "How Data Can Make Better Managers," *Harvard Business Review*, March 2, 2022, https://hbr.org/2022/03/how-data-can-make-better-managers.

5. Kevin Cashman and David Dotlich, "Leadership Development: CEOs' Strategic Powerhouse," *Korn Ferry*, September 23, 2015, https://www.kornferry.com/insights/this-week-in-leadership/leadership-development-ceos-strategic-powerhouse.

6. Gartner, "Gartner Survey Shows Only Half of Business Leaders Feel Confident Leading Their Teams Today," news release, July 23, 2019, https://www.gartner.com/en/newsroom/press-releases/2019-07-22-gartner-survey-shows-only-half-of-business-leaders-fe.

7. Edelman, "Edelman Trust Barometer: Societal Leadership Is Now a Core Function of Business," January 18, 2022, https://www.edelman.com/trust/2022-trust-barometer.

8. Bernd Vogel et al., "A Bibliometric Review of the Leadership Development Field: How We Got Here, Where We Are, and Where We Are Headed," *Leadership Quarterly* 32, no. 5 (2021): 101381, https://doi.org/10.1016/j.leaqua.2020.101381.

9. Paul Joseph-Richard, Gareth Edwards, and Shirley-Ann Hazlett, "Leadership Development Outcomes Research and the Need for a Time-Sensitive Approach," *Human Resource Development International* 24, no. 2 (2021): 173–199.

10. Day and Dragoni, *Leadership Development*, 133–156.

11. Robert Hogan, Robert Raskin, and Dan Fazzini, "The Dark Side of Charisma," in *Measures of Leadership*, ed. by Kenneth E. Clark and Miriam B. Clark (West Orange, NJ: Leadership Library of America, 1990), 343–354.

12. Vogel et al., *Bibliometric Review* (see note 6).

13. Vogel et al., *Bibliometric Review*.

14. Martin Rogers, "Sports Science Making Athletes Happier, Healthier and Stronger," *Fox Sport*, March 26, 2021, https://www.foxsports.com/stories/mlb/sports-science-happier-healther-stronger-athlete-martin-rogers.

15. John Antonakis, "Leadership to Defeat COVID-19," *Group Processes & Intergroup Relations* 24, no. 2 (2021): 210–215.

16. Robert Hogan et al., "Twenty Years on the Dark Side: Six Lessons about Bad Leadership," *Consulting Psychology Journal: Practice and Research* 73, no. 3 (2021): 199–213.

17. "Measuring Leadership Development," *Training*, May 10, 2019, https://trainingmag.com/measuring-leadership-development/.

18. "Five Ways to Improve Your Employee Experience," Virgin Media O2 Insights, March 29, 2022, https://www.virginmediao2business.co.uk/insights/improve-employee-experience/.

19. Kevin Kruse, "How Associa Turns Competencies into Behaviors through Leadership Development," *Forbes*, March 25, 2022, https://www.forbes.com/sites/kevinkruse/2022/03/25/how-associa-turns-competencies-into-behaviors-through-leadership-development/.

20. Anish Mukker, "Living the Amazon Leadership Principles through Catapult: A Leadership Development Initiative," Harvard Business Publishing Corporate Learning, October 11, 2021, https://www.harvard-business.org/living-the-amazon-leadership-principles-through-catapult-a-leadership-development-initiative/.

21. Rachel Osikoya, "How We Can Use Tech to Improve Diversity in the Workplace," World Economic Forum, June 23, 2020, https://www.weforum.org/agenda/2020/06/technology-ally-inclusion-diversity-work/.

22. Douglas Broom, "This is the Most Important Skill for a Leader to Have Right Now," World Economic Forum, October 11, 2021, https://www.weforum.org/agenda/2021/10/secret-great-leadership-empathy/.

23. Tara Van Bommel, "The Power of Empathy in Times of Crisis and Beyond," Catalyst, June 29, 2022, https://www.catalyst.org/reports/empathy-work-strategy-crisis.

24. Anna Webber, "Empathetic Leadership: The Key to Employee Retention," TeamBonding, October 14, 2021, https://www.teambonding.com/empathetic-leadership-the-key-to-employee-retention/.

25. Harvey Deutschendorf, "5 Reasons Empathy is Becoming the Number One Leadership Skill," RealLeaders, May 13, 2021, https://real-leaders.com/5-reasons-empathy-is-becoming-the-number-one-leadership-skill/.

26. Vivian Acquah, "Using VR to Unlock Empathy," AmplifyDEI, November 20, 2021, https://amplifydei.com/using-vr-to-unlock-empathy/.

27. Chris N. W. Geraets et al., "Virtual Reality Facial Emotion Recognition in Social Environments: An Eye-tracking Study." *Internet Interventions* 25 (2021): 100432, https://doi.org/10.1016/j.invent.2021.100432.

28. Mark H. Davis, "Measuring Individual Differences in Empathy: Evidence for a Multidimensional Approach," *Journal of Personality and Social Psychology* 44, no. 1 (1983): 113–126.

29. Tim Laseter, "The Line between Confidence and Hubris," Strategy+Business, November 21, 2016, https://www.strategy-business.com/article/The-Line-between-Confidence-and-Hubris.

30. Adrian R. Camilleri, "Overconfidence Is Responsible for a Lot of Mistakes, Here's How to Avoid It," The Conversation, July 18, 2016, https://the-conversation.com/overconfidence-is-responsible-for-a-lot-of-mistakes-heres-how-to-avoid-it-61907.

31. Ruth H. Axelrod, "Leadership and Self Confidence," in *Leadership Today: Practices for Personal and Professional Performance*, ed. by Joan Marques and Satinder Dhiman (New York: Springer, 2016), 297–313.

32. "Platform," Bodyswaps, accessed November 4, 2022, https://bodyswaps.co/corporate/.

33. Mike Gualtieri, "Hadoop Is Data's Darling for a Reason," Forrester, January 21, 2016, https://www.forrester.com/blogs/hadoop-is-datas-darling-for-a-reason/.

34. "Professional Data Engineer," Google Cloud, accessed November 4, 2022, https://cloud.google.com/certification/data-engineer.

35. "What is Data Science?" Oracle, accessed November 4, 2022, https://www.oracle.com/what-is-data-science/#defined.

36. "IBM Leadership, Learning, and Inclusion," IBM, accessed November 4, 2022, https://www.ibm.com/case-studies/ibm-leadership-learning-inclusion-manager-engagement.

CHAPTER 2: RELEASING THE DEI TALENT RIVER

1. Sundiatu Dixon-Fyle et al., "Diversity Wins: How Inclusion Matters," McKinsey & Company (2020), https://www.mckinsey.com/~/media/mckinsey/featured%20insights/diversity%20and%20inclusion/diversity%20wins%20how%20inclusion%20matters/diversity-wins-how-inclusion-matters-vf.pdf.

2. Deloitte, "The Chief Executive Program: Winter 2022 Fortune/Deloitte CEO Survey," (2022), https://www2.deloitte.com/content/dam/Deloitte/us/Documents/about-deloitte/us-fortune-deloitte-CEO-survey-winter-2022-highlights-final.pdf.

3. Deloitte, "The Chief Executive Program: Fall 2022 Fortune/Deloitte CEO Survey" (2022), https://www2.deloitte.com/us/en/pages/chief-executive-officer/articles/ceo-survey.html.

4. Sundiatu Dixon-Fyle et al., "Diversity Wins," https://www.mckinsey.com/~/media/mckinsey/featured%20insights/diversity%20and%20inclusion/diversity%20wins%20how%20inclusion%20matters/diversity-wins-how-inclusion-matters-vf.pdf.

5. Edelman, "Trust Barometer Special Report: Brand Trust in 2020," June 25, 2020, https://www.edelman.com/research/brand-trust-2020.

6. European Commission, "Eurobarometer 2022: EU Citizens Strongly Support International Cooperation to Reduce Poverty and Build Partnerships with Partner Countries," June 20, 2022, https://www. pubaffairsbruxelles.eu/eu-institution-news/eurobarometer-2022-eu-citizens-strongly-support-international-cooperation-to-reduce-poverty-and-build-partnerships-with-partner-countries/.

7. European Commission, "Global Gateway," accessed November 9, 2022, https://ec.europa.eu/info/strategy/priorities-2019-2024/stronger-europe-world/global-gateway_en.

8. Abby Kiesa, "More Young Voters Could Come Out to Vote in November, Sparked by Abortion and Other Hot Political Issues," The Conversation, July 15, 2022, https://theconversation.com/more-young-voters-could-come-out-to-vote-in-november-sparked-by-abortion-and-other-hot-political-issues-186802.

9. Quinetta M. Roberson, "Diversity in the Workplace: A Review, Synthesis, and Future Research Agenda." *Annual Review of Organizational Psychology and Organizational Behavior* 6 (2019): 70, https://www.annualreviews.org/doi/abs/10.1146/annurev-orgpsych-012218-015243.

10. Paula, Braveman and Sofia Gruskin, "Defining Equity in Health." *Journal of Epidemiology & Community Health* 57, no. 4 (2003): 254, https://jech.bmj.com/content/57/4/254.short.

11. Michal E. Mor-Barak, and David A. Cherin, "A Tool to Expand Organizational Understanding of Workforce Diversity: Exploring a Measure of Inclusion-Exclusion." *Administration in Social Work* 22, no. 1 (1998): 48, https://www.tandfonline.com/doi/pdf/10.1300/J147v22n01_04?casa_token=vUh9Z5jyHIYAAAAA:1AgDXCTezH82AuZL5zN0V-vf-gilx5gG2a1yLJmxJYPQupZL7Jlrz9ohNqKnjX9Nx5D6SA5cn3y5.

12. Harvard Business Review Analytic Services, "Creating a Culture of Diversity, Equity, and Inclusion: Real Progress Requires Sustained Commitment," (2021), https://www.shrm.org/hr-today/trends-and-forecasting/research-and-surveys/Documents/DEI%20Metrics%20Full%20Report.pdf.

13. Quinetta M. Roberson, *Diversity in the Workplace*, 69–88.

14. Jeffrey Davis, "The Bias Against Difference and How It Gets in the Way of Creativity and Collaboration," *Psychology Today*, June 25, 2020, https://www.psychologytoday.com/us/blog/tracking-wonder/202006/the-bias-against-difference.

15. Brian R. Spisak, "How Data Can Make Better Managers," *Harvard Business Review*, March 2, 2022, https://hbr.org/2022/03/how-data-can-make-better-managers.

16. Brian R. Spisak et al., "A Face for All Seasons: Searching for Context-Specific Leadership Traits and Discovering a General Preference for Perceived Health." *Frontiers in Human Neuroscience* 8 (2014): 1–9, https://www.frontiersin.org/articles/10.3389/fnhum.2014.00792/full.

17. Quinetta M. Roberson, *Diversity in the Workplace*, 69–88.

18. Kelsey McKeon, "How to Develop an Employer Branding Strategy in 2020," The Manifest, June 18, 2020, https://themanifest.com/digital-marketing/employer-branding-strategy-2020#h2-10.

19. Maggie Overfelt, "Hey, Employers: Job Hunters Really Want to See Your Diversity Data," *Stanford Business Insight*, March 21, 2022, https://www.gsb.stanford.edu/insights/hey-employers-job-hunters-really-want-see-your-diversity-data.

20. Juliet Bourke, "The Diversity and Inclusion Revolution: Eight Powerful Truths," *Deloitte Review*, January 22, 2018, https://www2.deloitte.com/us/en/insights/deloitte-review/issue-22/diversity-and-inclusion-at-work-eight-powerful-truths.html.

21. World Economic Forum, "Diversity, Equity and Inclusion 4.0: A Toolkit for Leaders to Accelerate Social Progress in the Future of Work," June 23, 2020, https://www.weforum.org/reports/diversity-equity-and-inclusion-4-0-a-toolkit-for-leaders-to-accelerate-social-progress-in-the-future-of-work/.

22. Quinetta M. Roberson, *Diversity in the Workplace*, 69–88.

23. "Google Programmable Search Engine," accessed November 9, 2022, https://programmablesearchengine.google.com/about/.

24. Yuma Heymans, "Sourcing Talent with the Programmable Search Engine (PSE)," HeroHunt.ai, July 26, 2021, https://www.herohunt.ai/blog/the-complete-guide-to-recruiting-talent-with-the-google-programmable-search-engine-pse.

25. World Economic Forum, *Diversity, Equity and Inclusion 4.0*, June 23, 2020.

26. Tomi Akitunde, "What Can AI Teach Us about Empathy?," Dropbox Work in Progress blog, December 10, 2021, https://blog.dropbox.com/topics/work-culture/what-can-ai-teach-us-about-empathy-.

27. Joseph Stromberg and Estelle Caswell, "Why the Myers-Briggs Test is Totally Meaningless," *Vox*, October 8, 2015, https://www.vox.com/2014/7/15/5881947/myers-briggs-personality-test-meaningless#:~:text=The%20Myers%2DBriggs%20provides%20inconsistent%2C%20inaccurate%20results&text=Research%20has%20found%20that%20as, it's%20just%20five%20weeks%20later.&text=That's%20because%20the%20traits%20it,are%20consistently%20different%20among%20people.

28. James Vincent, "Automated Hiring Software Is Mistakenly Rejecting Millions of Viable Job Candidates," *The Verge*, September 6, 2021, https://www.theverge.com/2021/9/6/22659225/automated-hiring-software-rejecting-viable-candidates-harvard-business-school.

29. "The HR Machine," accessed November 9, 2022, https://www.thehrmachine.com/.

30. "Chicago Equity Dashboard," accessed November 9, 2022, https://www.chicago.gov/city/en/sites/office-of-equity-and-racial-justice/home/dashboard.html.

31. "MIT Diversity Dashboard," accessed November 9, 2022, https://ir.mit.edu/diversity-dashboard/.

32. Maya Bodan, Devon Dickau, and India Mullady, "Using Adaptable Organization Network Analysis to Reveal Patterns that Drive Inclusion," Deloitte, April, 21, 2020, https://www2.deloitte.com/us/en/blog/human-capital-blog/2020/using-adaptable-organization-network-analysis-to-reveal-patterns-that-drive-inclusion.html.

33. Ibid.

34. HSC Analytics, accessed November 9, 2022, https://www.hscanalytics.com/.

35. Ibid.

36. "How does Swarm Work?" Unanimous AI, accessed November 9, 2022, https://unanimous.ai/what-is-si/.

37. Rutwik Shah, "Using a Digital Swarm® Platform to Improve Consensus among Radiologists," Center for Intelligent Imagining, November 22, 2021, https://intelligentimaging.ucsf.edu/news/using-digital-swarmr-platform-improve-consensus-among-radiologists.

CHAPTER 3: BREAKING THE DEATH-BY-MEETINGS CURSE AND OTHER ENGAGEMENT KILLERS

1. "PwC Pulse Survey: Executive Views on Business in 2022," PwC, January 27, 2022, https://www.pwc.com/us/en/library/pulse-survey/executive-views-2022.html.

2. Jackie Wiles, "CEOs Turn a Sharp Eye to Workforce Issues and Sustainability in 2022-23," Gartner, April 27, 2022, https://www.gartner.com/en/articles/ceos-turn-a-sharp-eye-to-workforce-issues-and-sustainability-in-2022-23.

3. James K. Harter et al., "The Relationship Between Engagement at Work and Organizational Outcomes," Gallup, October 13, 2020, https://www.gallup.com/workplace/321725/gallup-q12-meta-analysis-report.aspx.

4. Arnold B. Bakker and Simon Albrecht, "Work Engagement: Current Trends," *Career Development International* 23, no. 1 (2018): 4–11, https://www.emerald.com/insight/content/doi/10.1108/CDI-11-2017-0207/full/html.

5. Jason C Gawke, Marjan J. Gorgievski, and Arnold B. Bakker, "Employee Intrapreneurship and Work Engagement: A Latent Change Score Approach," *Journal of Vocational Behavior* 100 (2017): 88–100, https://www.sciencedirect.com/science/article/pii/S0001879117300209.

6. Maximilian Orth and Judith Volmer, "Daily Within-Person Effects of Job Autonomy and Work Engagement on Innovative Behaviour: The Cross-Level Moderating Role of Creative Self-Efficacy," *European Journal of Work and Organizational Psychology* 26, no. 4 (2017): 601–612, https://www.tandfonline.com/doi/abs/10.1080/1359432X.2017.1332042.

7. Patrícia L. Costa, Ana M. Passos, and Arnold B. Bakker, "Direct and Contextual Influence of Team Conflict on Team Resources, Team Work Engagement, and Team Performance," *Negotiation and Conflict Management Research* 8, no. 4 (2015): 211–227, https://onlinelibrary.wiley.com/doi/abs/10.1111/ncmr.12061.

8. Maria Tims et al., "Job Crafting at the Team and Individual Level: Implications for Work Engagement and Performance," *Group & Organization Management* 38, no. 4 (2013): 427–454, https://journals.sagepub.com/doi/abs/10.1177/1059601113492421.

9. Jari J. Hakanen, Petri Rouvinen, and Ilkka Ylhäinen, "The Impact of Work Engagement on Future Occupational Rankings, Wages, Unemployment, and Disability Pensions—A Register-Based Study of a Representative Sample of Finnish Employees," *Sustainability* 13, no. 4 (2021): 1626, https://www.mdpi.com/2071-1050/13/4/1626.

10. Jim Harter, "U.S. Employee Engagement Slump Continues," Gallup, April 25, 2022, https://www.gallup.com/workplace/391922/employee-engagement-slump-continues.aspx.

11. James K. Harter et al., "The Relationship Between Engagement at Work and Organizational Outcomes," October 13, 2020, https://www.mandalidis.ch/coaching/2021/01/2020-employee-engagement-meta-analysis.pdf.

12. Arnold B. Bakker et al., "Work Engagement: An Emerging Concept in Occupational Health Psychology," *Work & Stress* 22, no. 3 (2008): 187, https://www.tandfonline.com/doi/abs/10.1080/02678370802393649.

13. Henry R. Young et al., "Who are the Most Engaged at Work? A Meta-Analysis of Personality and Employee Engagement," *Journal of Organizational Behavior* 39, no. 10 (2018): 1330–1346, https://onlinelibrary.wiley.com/doi/abs/10.1002/job.2303.

14. M. Ryan Richard and L. Deci Edward. "Self-Determination Theory and the Facilitation of Intrinsic Motivation, Social Development, and Well-Being," *American Psychologist* 55, no. 1 (2000): 68–78, https://psycnet.apa.org/doiLanding?doi=10.1037%2F0003-066X.55.1.68.

15. James K. Harter et al., "The Relationship Between Engagement at Work and Organizational Outcomes," October 13, 2020, https://www.mandalidis.ch/coaching/2021/01/2020-employee-engagement-meta-analysis.pdf.

16. "People Management: Pros, Cons and Development Opportunities," Gallup, accessed November 11, 2022, https://www.gallup.com/workplace/321074/perks-and-challenges-of-management.aspx#ite-321086.

17. "Workplace Burnout Survey: Burnout Without Borders," Deloitte, accessed November 11, 2022, https://www2.deloitte.com/us/en/pages/about-deloitte/articles/burnout-survey.html.

18. Nina M. Junker et al., "Is Work Engagement Exhausting? The Longitudinal Relationship between Work Engagement and Exhaustion Using Latent Growth Modeling," *Applied Psychology* 70, no. 2 (2021): 788-815, https://iaap-journals.onlinelibrary.wiley.com/doi/full/10.1111/apps.12252.

19. Alan M. Saks and Jamie A. Gruman, "Socialization Resources Theory and Newcomers' Work Engagement: A New Pathway to Newcomer Socialization," *Career Development International* 23, no. 1 (2018): 12–32, https://www.emerald.com/insight/content/doi/10.1108/CDI-12-2016-0214/full/html.

20. Greta Mazzetti et al., "Work Engagement: A Meta-Analysis Using the Job Demands-Resources Model," *Psychological Reports* (2021): 00332941211051988, https://journals.sagepub.com/doi/abs/10.1177/00332941211051988.

21. Tino Lesener et al., "The Drivers of Work Engagement: A Meta-Analytic Review of Longitudinal Evidence," *Work & Stress* 34, no. 3 (2020): 259–278, https://www.tandfonline.com/doi/abs/10.1080/02678373.2019.1686440.

22. Jennifer R. Burnett and Timothy C. Lisk, "The Future of Employee Engagement: Real-Time Monitoring and Digital Tools for Engaging a Workforce," *International Studies of Management & Organization* 49, no. 1 (2019): 108–119, https://www.tandfonline.com/doi/abs/10.1080/00208825.2019.1565097.

23. Vivi Gusrini Rahmadani, Wilmar B. Schaufeli, and Jeroen Stouten. "How Engaging Leaders Foster Employees' Work Engagement," *Leadership & Organization Development Journal* 41, no. 8 (2020): 1155–1169, https://

www.emerald.com/insight/content/doi/10.1108/LODJ-01-2020-0014/full/html.

24. Jay L. Caulfield and Anthony Senger, "Perception Is Reality: Change Leadership and Work Engagement," *Leadership and Organization Development Journal* 38, no. 7 (2017): 927–945, https://www.emerald.com/insight/content/doi/10.1108/LODJ-07-2016-0166/full/html?fullSc=1.

25. Francis J. Yammarino et al., "Collectivistic Leadership Approaches: Putting the 'We' in Leadership Science and Practice," *Industrial and Organizational Psychology* 5, no. 4 (2012): 382–402, https://www.cambridge.org/core/journals/industrial-and-organizational-psychology/article/abs/collectivistic-leadership-approaches-putting-the-we-in-leadership-science-and-practice/9D83C1BEEA6607A28F1C1686B0533C9C.

26. Arnold B. Bakker, Evangelia Demerouti, and Ana Isabel Sanz-Vergel, "Burnout and Work Engagement: The JD–R Approach," *Annual Review of Organizational Psychology and Organizational Behavior* 1, no. 1 (2014): 389–411, https://www.annualreviews.org/doi/abs/10.1146/annurev-orgpsych-031413-091235.

27. Annamarie Mann and Nate Dvorak, "Employee Recognition: Low Cost, High Impact," Gallup, June 28, 2016, https://www.gallup.com/workplace/236441/employee-recognition-low-cost-high-impact.aspx.

28. Ashley Bell, "The Best Employee Recognition Software Platforms and Reward Programs Used by Notable Companies In 2022," SnackNation, October 12, 2022, https://snacknation.com/blog/employee-recognition-software/.

29. Joseph Stromberg and Estelle Caswell, "Why the Myers-Briggs Test is Totally Meaningless," *Vox*, October 8, 2015, https://www.vox.com/2014/7/15/5881947/myers-briggs-personality-test-meaningless.

30. James Vincent, "Automated Hiring Software is Mistakenly Rejecting Millions of Viable Job Candidates," *The Verge*, September 6, 2021, https://www.theverge.com/2021/9/6/22659225/automated-hiring-software-rejecting-viable-candidates-harvard-business-school.

31. Cem Dilmegani, "In-Depth Guide into Applicant Tracking Systems (ATS) in 2022," AI Multiple, September 12, 2022, https://research.aimultiple.com/ats/.

32. Daria Zabój, "Key Chatbot Statistics You Should Follow in 2022," ChatBot, July 12, 2022, https://www.chatbot.com/blog/chatbot-statistics/.

33. Talya N. Bauer, "Onboarding New Employees: Maximizing Success," *SHRM Foundation's Effective Practice Guidelines Series* (2010), https://www.shrm.org/foundation/ourwork/initiatives/resources-from-past-initiatives/

Documents/Onboarding%20New%20Employees.pdf?utm_source=link_wwwv9&utm_campaign=item_235121&utm_medium=copy.

34. Arlene S. Hirsch, "Don't Underestimate the Importance of Good Onboarding," Society for Human Resource Management, August 10, 2017, https://www.shrm.org/resourcesandtools/hr-topics/talent-acquisition/pages/dont-underestimate-the-importance-of-effective-onboarding.aspx.

35. Madeline Laurano, "The True Cost of a Bad Hire," Brandon Hall Group (2015), https://b2b-assets.glassdoor.com/the-true-cost-of-a-bad-hire.pdf.

36. Julie Cook Ramirez, "These New Technologies Are Transforming Mentoring Programs," *Human Resource Executive*, January 9, 2019, https://hrexecutive.com/these-new-technologies-are-transforming-mentoring-programs/.

37. Susan Galer, "AI-Based Career Mentoring for the Masses: When People Talk, Innovation Happens," *Forbes*, June 25, 2019, https://www.forbes.com/sites/sap/2019/06/25/ai-based-career-mentoring-for-the-masses-when-people-talk-innovation-happens/?sh=714a36e476d1.

38. Jeanne C. Meister, "How Deloitte Made Learning a Game," *Harvard Business Review*, January 2, 2013, https://hbr.org/2013/01/how-deloitte-made-learning-a-g.

39. Fares Laroui, "The State of Gamification in the Workplace: Use Cases and Future Trends," eXo, February 27, 2020, https://www.exoplatform.com/blog/gamification-in-the-workplace-use-cases-and-future-trends-exo-platform/.

40. Human Resource Analytics, hscanalytics.com, accessed November 11, 2022, https://www.hscanalytics.com/.

41. Ben Laker et al., "The Surprising Impact of Meeting-Free Days," *MIT Sloan Management Review*, January 18, 2022, https://sloanreview.mit.edu/article/the-surprising-impact-of-meeting-free-days/.

42. Fabrice Lumineau et al., "How Blockchain Can Simplify Partnerships," *Harvard Business Review*, April 9, 2021, https://hbr.org/2021/04/how-blockchain-can-simplify-partnerships.

43. OneTen, oneten.org, accessed November 11, 2022, https://oneten.org/.

CHAPTER 4: MASTERING THE BUBBLES AND TIGHTROPES OF SUSTAINABILITY

1. J. David Rogers et al., "Interaction between the US Army Corps of Engineers and the Orleans Levee Board Preceding the Drainage Canal Wall Failures and Catastrophic Flooding of New Orleans in 2005," *Water*

Policy 17, no. 4 (2015): 707–723, https://iwaponline.com/wp/article/17/4/707/20452/Interaction-between-the-US-Army-Corps-of-Engineers.

2. Martin Conyon, William Q. Judge, and Michael Useem, "Corporate Governance and the 2008–09 Financial Crisis," *Corporate Governance: An International Review* 19, no. 5 (2011): 399–404, https://onlinelibrary.wiley.com/doi/full/10.1111/j.1467-8683.2011.00879.x.

3. Emilie Alirol et al., "Urbanisation and Infectious Diseases in a Globalised World," *The Lancet Infectious Diseases* 11, no. 2 (2011): 131–141, https://www.sciencedirect.com/science/article/pii/S1473309910702231.

4. Yang, X. Jin. "China's Rapid Urbanization," *Science* 342, no. 6156 (2013): 310–310, https://www.science.org/doi/abs/10.1126/science.342.6156.310-a.

5. Cameron Zachreson et al., "Urbanization Affects Peak Timing, Prevalence, and Bimodality of Influenza Pandemics in Australia: Results of a Census-Calibrated Model," *Science Advances* 4, no. 12 (2018): eaau5294, https://www.science.org/doi/10.1126/sciadv.aau5294.

6. Gerald T. Keusch et al., "Pandemic Origins and a One Health Approach to Preparedness and Prevention: Solutions Based on SARS-CoV-2 and other RNA Viruses," *Proceedings of the National Academy of Sciences* 119, no. 42 (2022): e2202871119, https://www.pnas.org/doi/full/10.1073/pnas.2202871119.

7. Francesc Romagosa, "The COVID-19 Crisis: Opportunities for Sustainable and Proximity Tourism," *Tourism Geographies* 22, no. 3 (2020): 690–694, https://www.tandfonline.com/doi/full/10.1080/14616688.2020.1763447.

8. Ruiyun Li et al., "Substantial Undocumented Infection Facilitates the Rapid Dissemination of Novel Coronavirus (SARS-CoV-2)," *Science* 368, no. 6490 (2020): 489–493, https://www.science.org/doi/full/10.1126/science.abb3221.

9. Jahidur Rahman Khan et al., "Healthcare Capacity, Health Expenditure, and Civil Society as Predictors of COVID-19 Case Fatalities: A Global Analysis," *Frontiers in Public Health* 8 (2020): 1–10, https://www.frontiersin.org/articles/10.3389/fpubh.2020.00347/full.

10. Jan Osička and Filip Černoch, "European Energy Politics after Ukraine: The Road Ahead," *Energy Research & Social Science* 91 (2022): 102757, https://www.sciencedirect.com/science/article/pii/S2214629622002602.

11. George A. Bray and Barry M. Popkin, "Dietary Sugar and Body Weight: Have We Reached a Crisis in the Epidemic of Obesity and Diabetes? Health be Damned! Pour on the Sugar," *Diabetes Care* 37, no. 4 (2014): 950–956, https://diabetesjournals.org/care/article/37/4/950/32201/Dietary-Sugar-and-Body-Weight-Have-We-Reached-a.

12. David S. Ludwig and Marion Nestle, "Can the Food Industry Play a Constructive Role in the Obesity Epidemic?," *JAMA* 300, no. 15 (2008): 1808–1811, https://jamanetwork.com/journals/jama/article-abstract/182715.

13. "Company ESG Risk Ratings, Accenture Plc," Sustainalytics, accessed November 10, 2022, https://www.sustainalytics.com/esg-rating/accenture-plc/1008850436.

14. "Accenture's 360° Value Reporting Experience," Accenture, accessed November 10, 2022, https://www.accenture.com/us-en/about/company/integrated-reporting.

15. Ibid.

16. "United National Sustainable Development Goals," United National Department of Economic and Social Affairs, accessed November 10, 2022, https://sdgs.un.org/goals.

17. UN News Centre, "Sustainable Development Goals Kick off with Start of New Year," United Nations, December 30, 2015, https://www.un.org/sustainabledevelopment/blog/2015/12/sustainable-development-goals-kick-off-with-start-of-new-year/.

18. Wendy Stubbs and Chris Cocklin, "Conceptualizing a 'Sustainability Business Model'," *Organization & Environment* 21, no. 2 (2008): 103–127, https://journals.sagepub.com/doi/abs/10.1177/1086026608318042.

19. EY Americas, "How to Embrace Sustainable Supply Chains to Secure Long-Term Value," EY, March 17, 2021, https://www.ey.com/en_us/supply-chain/how-to-embrace-sustainable-supply-chains-to-secure-long-term-value.

20. Better Business, Better World Report, "Sustainable Business can Unlock at Least $12 Trillion in New Market Value and Repair the Economic System," Business and Sustainable Development Commission, January 16, 2017, https://businesscommission.org/news/release-sustainable-business-can-unlock-at-least-us-12-trillion-in-new-market-value-and-repair-economic-system.

21. "G20 Countries," The Energy Policy Tracker, December 31, 2021, https://www.energypolicytracker.org/region/g20/.

22. "Global Sustainable Investment Review 2020," Global Sustainable Investment Alliance (2020), http://www.gsi-alliance.org/wp-content/uploads/2021/08/GSIR-20201.pdf.

23. Magali A. Delmas and Sanja Pekovic, "Environmental Standards and Labor Productivity: Understanding the Mechanisms that Sustain Sustainability," *Journal of Organizational Behavior* 34, no. 2 (2013): 230–252, https://onlinelibrary.wiley.com/doi/10.1002/job.1827.

24. IBM Institute for Business Value, "Sustainability at a Turning Point, Consumers are Pushing Companies to Pivot," IBM (2021), https://www.ibm.com/downloads/cas/WLJ7LVP4.

25. "Recent Study Reveals More Than a Third of Global Consumers Are Willing to Pay More for Sustainability as Demand Grows for Environmentally-Friendly Alternatives," Simon-Kucher & Partners, October 25, 2021, https://www.simon-kucher.com/en/about/media-center/recent-study-reveals-more-third-global-consumers-are-willing-pay-more-sustainability-demand-grows-environmentally-friendly-alternatives.

26. Jackie Wiles, "CEOs Turn a Sharp Eye to Workforce Issues and Sustainability in 2022–23," Gartner, April 27, 2022, https://www.gartner.com/en/articles/ceos-turn-a-sharp-eye-to-workforce-issues-and-sustainability-in-2022-23.

27. "PwC's 25th Annual Global CEO Survey, Reimagining the Outcomes that Matter," PwC, January 17, 2022, https://www.pwc.com/gx/en/ceo-agenda/ceosurvey/2022.html.

28. "IBM Study: Sustainability Ranks Among Highest Priorities on CEO Agendas, Yet Lack of Data Insights Hinders Progress," IBM, May 10, 2022, https://newsroom.ibm.com/2022-05-10-IBM-Study-CEOs-Feel-Pressure-to-Act-on-Sustainability-and-See-Business-Benefits,-Yet-Hindered-by-Challenges.

29. Adele Peters, "68% of U.S. Execs Admit Their Companies are Guilty of Greenwashing," *Fast Company*, April, 14, 2022, https://www.fastcompany.com/90740501/68-of-u-s-execs-admit-their-companies-are-guilty-of-greenwashing.

30. Economic Research Service, "Statistics & Information for the Most Current Coverage of U.S. Livestock Outlook," US Department Of Agriculture, accessed November 10, 2022, https://www.ers.usda.gov/topics/animal-products/cattle-beef/statistics-information/.

31. Willem Roper, "Beef: It's What's Contributing to Climate Change," Statista, August 3 2020, https://www.statista.com/chart/22450/meat-production-and-climate-change/.

32. "$99 Billion Worldwide Fast Fashion Industry Report to 2031: Identify Growth Segments for Investment—ResearchAndMarkets.com," Business Wire, April 20, 2022, https://www.businesswire.com/news/home/20220420005724/en/99-Billion-Worldwide-Fast-Fashion-Industry-Report-to-2031---Identify-Growth-Segments-for-Investment---ResearchAndMarkets.com.

33. Yasaman Yousefi, "Environmental and Social Impacts of Fast Fashion," SDWatch, February 18, 2020, https://sdwatch.eu/2020/02/environmental-and-social-impacts-of-fast-fashion/.

34. Michele Micheletti and Andreas Follesdal, "Shopping for Human Rights. An Introduction to the Special Issue," *Journal of Consumer Policy* 30, no. 3 (2007): 167–175, https://link.springer.com/article/10.1007/s10603-007-9039-0.

35. Liz Szabo, "Big Soda and the Ballot: Soda Industry Takes Cues from Tobacco to Combat Taxes," NPR, November 5, 2018, https://www.npr.org/sections/thesalt/2018/11/05/664435761/big-soda-and-the-ballot-soda-industry-takes-cues-from-tobacco-to-combat-taxes.

36. Alvin Powell, "Tracing Big Oil's PR War to Delay Action on Climate Change," *The Harvard Gazette*, September 28, 2021, https://news.harvard.edu/gazette/story/2021/09/oil-companies-discourage-climate-action-study-says/.

37. "10 Things to Know about Big Tobacco's Arts Sponsorship," STOP, December 16, 2021, https://exposetobacco.org/news/big-tobacco-arts-sponsorship/.

38. Jack Ewing, "Volkswagen Will Seek Damages from Former Executives Accused in Emissions Fraud," *The New York Times*, March 26, 2021, https://www.nytimes.com/2021/03/26/business/volkswagen-emissions-winterkorn-stadler.html.

39. David Young and Martin Reeves, "The Quest for Sustainable Business Model Innovation," BCG Henderson Institute, March 20, 2020, https://web-assets.bcg.com/img-src/BCG-The-Quest-for-Sustainable-Business-Model-Innovation-Mar-2020_tcm9-240570.pdf.

40. Amanda Schupak, "Is Remote Working Better for the Environment? Not Necessarily," *The Guardian*, August 2, 2021, https://www.theguardian.com/environment/2021/aug/02/is-remote-working-better-for-the-environment-not-necessarily.

41. Minmin Shen and Jianhua Wang, "The Impact of Pro-Environmental Awareness Components on Green Consumption Behavior: The Moderation Effect of Consumer Perceived Cost, Policy Incentives, and Face Culture," *Frontiers in Psychology* 13 (2022): 580823, https://www.ncbi.nlm.nih.gov/pmc/articles/PMC9252608/.

42. Manjana Milkoreit et al, "Defining Tipping Points for Social-Ecological Systems Scholarship: An Interdisciplinary Literature Review," *Environmental Research Letters* 13, no. 3 (2018): 033005, https://iopscience.iop.org/article/10.1088/1748-9326/aaaa75/meta.

43. Ilona M. Otto et al., "Social Tipping Dynamics for Stabilizing Earth's Climate by 2050," *Proceedings of the National Academy of Sciences* 117, no. 5 (2020): 2354–2365, https://www.pnas.org/doi/10.1073/pnas.1900577117.

44. James G. March, "Exploration and Exploitation in Organizational Learning." *Organization Science* 2, no. 1 (1991): 71–87, https://pubsonline. informs.org/doi/abs/10.1287/orsc.2.1.71.

45. Brian R. Spisak et al., "The Age of Exploration and Exploitation: Younger-Looking Leaders Endorsed for Change and Older-Looking Leaders Endorsed for Stability." *The Leadership Quarterly* 25, no. 5 (2014): 805–816, https://www.sciencedirect.com/science/article/pii/S1048984314000605.

46. Brian R. Spisak et al., *The Age of Exploration and Exploitation*, 805–816.

47. Tuomo Peltonen, *Towards Wise Management: Wisdom and Stupidity in Strategic Decision-Making* (Cham: Palgrave Macmillan, 2019).

48. Quy Huy and Timo Vuori, "Who Killed Nokia? Nokia Did," INSEAD, September 22, 2015, https://knowledge.insead.edu/strategy/who-killed-nokia-nokia-did.

49. David Lee, "Nokia: The Rise and Fall of a Mobile Giant," *BBC News*, September 03, 2013, https://www.bbc.com/news/technology-23947212.

50. Taylor Bryant, "The Perfect Balance: How to Manage Inventory as Sustainably as Possible," EcoCart, November 23, 2021, https://ecocart.io/the-perfect-balance-how-to-manage-inventory-as-sustainably-as-possible/.

51. Brian R. Spisak, "Niche Construction and the Evolution of Leadership," *Academy of Management Review* 40, no. 2 (2015): 291–306, https://journals.aom.org/doi/abs/10.5465/amr.2013.0157.

52. Douglas W. S. Renwick, Tom Redman, and Stuart Maguire. "Green Human Resource Management: A Review and Research Agenda," *International Journal of Management Reviews* 15, no. 1 (2013): 1–14, https://onlinelibrary.wiley.com/doi/abs/10.1111/j.1468-2370.2011.00328.x.

53. Samuel Cunningham-Nelson, Mahsa Baktashmotlagh, and Wageeh Boles. "Visualizing Student Opinion through Text Analysis," *IEEE Transactions on Education* 62, no. 4 (2019): 305–311, https://ieeexplore.ieee.org/abstract/document/8759085.

54. Michael Saidani, Harrison Kim, and Bernard Yannou, "Can Machine Learning Tools Support the Identification of Sustainable Design Leads from Product Reviews? Opportunities and Challenges," in *International Design Engineering Technical Conferences and Computers and Information in Engineering Conference*, vol. 85383, p. V03AT03A005. American Society of Mechanical Engineers, 2021, https://arxiv.org/ftp/arxiv/papers/2112/2112.09391.pdf.

55. Michael Saidani et al., "Combining Life Cycle Assessment and Online Customer Reviews to Design More Sustainable Products: Case Study on

a Printing Machine," Procedia CIRP 109 (2022): 604–609, https://www.sciencedirect.com/science/article/pii/S2212827122007508.

56. Donald Lee Brown, "Using NLP to Gain Insights from Employee Review Data," Insight, March 28, 2019, https://blog.insightdatascience.com/using-nlp-to-gain-insights-from-employee-review-data-da15687f311a.

57. Anthony Leiserowitz et al., "International Public Opinion on Climate Change," Yale Program on Climate Change and Facebook Data for Good (2021), https://climatecommunication.yale.edu/wp-content/uploads/2021/06/international-climate-opinion-february-2021d.pdf.

58. Brian R. Spisak et al., "Large-Scale Decrease in the Social Salience of Climate Change During the COVID-19 Pandemic. *PLOS ONE* 17, no. 1 (2022): e0256082, https://journals.plos.org/plosone/article?id=10.1371/journal.pone.0256082.

59. David Hardisty, Rishad Habib, and Katherine White, "5 Ways to Shift Consumers towards Sustainable Behavior," GreenBiz, August, 21, 2019, https://www.greenbiz.com/article/5-ways-shift-consumers-towards-sustainable-behavior.

60. Yongsheng Zhang and Ilan Chabay, "How 'Green Knowledge' Influences Sustainability through Behavior Change: Theory and Policy Implications," *Sustainability* 12, no. 16 (2020): 6448, https://www.mdpi.com/2071-1050/12/16/6448.

61. Wil M. P. van der Aalst, "Process Mining: a 360 Degree Overview," in *Process Mining Handbook*, ed. by Wil M. P. van der Aalst and Josep Carmona (Cham: Springer, 2022), 3–34, https://doi.org/10.1007/978-3-031-08848-3_1.

62. Sanjay Podder and Shalabh Kumar Singh, "Tech + Sustainability = Leadership," Accenture, April 12, 2021, https://www.accenture.com/us-en/blogs/technology-innovation/tech-sustainability-leadership.

63. Nomoko, "The Era of Digital Twins and the Mirror World," *Medium*, May 5, 2020, https://nomoko.medium.com/the-era-of-digital-twins-and-the-mirror-world-82b33e3e3d46.

64. Stephen Moore, "Porsche in Joint Effort for Plastics Traceability," *Plastics Today*, November 10, 2020, https://www.plasticstoday.com/sustainability/porsche-joint-effort-plastics-traceability.

CHAPTER 5: LEADING THROUGH CRISIS, CRISIS, AND MORE CRISIS

1. Nataliya Kaster-Buchkovska, "The Consequences of the War in Ukraine Will Be Far-Reaching," World Economic Forum, April 29, 2022, https://

www.weforum.org/agenda/2022/04/an-unfair-war-economic-social-and-security-consequences-of-the-russian-invasion-into-ukraine/.

2. "PwC's Global Crisis Survey 2021," PwC Research, March 30, 2021, https://www.pwc.com/gx/en/issues/crisis-solutions/global-crisis-survey.html.

3. Uriel Rosenthal, Michael T. Charles, and Paul 't Hart, "Coping with Crises: The Management of Disasters, Riots, and Terrorism," in *Coping with Crises: The Management of Disasters, Riots, and Terrorism*, ed. by Uriel Rosenthal, Michael T. Charles, and Paul 't Hart (Springfield, IL: Charles C Thomas Pub Ltd, 1989), 10.

4. Dan Pyle Millar and Robert L. Heath, "A Rhetorical Approach to Crisis Communication: Management, Communication Processes, and Strategic Responses," in *Responding to Crisis*, ed. by Dan Pyle Millar and Robert L. Heath (New York: Routledge, 2003) 9-26, https://www.taylorfrancis.com/books/edit/10.4324/9781410609496/responding-crisis-dan-pyle-millar-robert-heath?refId=2710e945-0280-4ad7-abac-bf2629d2f076&context=ubx.

5. Jonathan Bundy et al., "Crises and Crisis Management: Integration, Interpretation, and Research Development," *Journal of Management* 43, no. 6 (2017): 1661–1692, https://journals.sagepub.com/doi/full/10.1177/0149206316680030.

6. Christine M. Pearson and Judith A. Clair, "Reframing Crisis Management," *Academy of Management Review* 23, no. 1 (1998): 59–76, https://journals.aom.org/doi/abs/10.5465/AMR.1998.192960.

7. Coombs, W. Timothy, *Ongoing Crisis Communication: Planning, Managing, and Responding* (Thousand Oaks, CA: Sage Publications, 2021), 5, https://us.sagepub.com/en-us/nam/ongoing-crisis-communication/book270207.

8. Timothy W. Coombs and Daniel Laufer, "Global Crisis Management: Current Research and Future Directions," *Journal of International Management* 24, no. 3 (2018): 199–203, https://www.sciencedirect.com/science/article/abs/pii/S1075425317304763.

9. Yuen Lam Wu et al, "Crisis Leadership: A Review and Future Research Agenda," *The Leadership Quarterly* 32, no. 6 (2021): 101518, https://www.sciencedirect.com/science/article/pii/S1048984321000230.

10. Leonard J. Marcus et al, *You're It: Crisis, Change, and How to Lead When It Matters Most* (New York: PublicAffairs, 2019), https://www.publicaffairsbooks.com/titles/leonard-j-marcus/youre-it/9781541768055/.

11. Governance Insight Center, "Turning Crisis into Opportunity: PwC's 2020 Annual Corporate Directors Survey," PwC (2020), http://www.circulodedirectores.org/wp-content/uploads/2021/03/pwc-2020-annual-corporate-directors-survey.pdf.

12. "Connected Crisis: In Search of Stability Amidst Chaos," Edelman (2022), https://www.edelman.com/sites/g/files/aatuss191/files/2022-09/2022%20Edelman%20Connected%20Crisis%20Study.pdf.

13. "Extreme Flood Events Once Again Drive High Losses in 2021, Yet 75% of Flood Risks Remain Uninsured, Swiss Re Institute Reveals," Swiss Re, March 30, 2022, https://www.swissre.com/press-release/Extreme-flood-events-once-again-drive-high-losses-in-2021-yet-75-of-flood-risks-remain-uninsured-Swiss-Re-Institute-reveals/3269ad99-b743-4398-82e3-534a87783910.

14. Steve Morgan, "Cybercrime to Cost the World $10.5 Trillion Annually by 2025," *Cybercrime Magazine*, November 13, 2020, https://cybersecurityventures.com/cybercrime-damages-6-trillion-by-2021/.

15. "Technological Hazards and Health Risks in Ukraine," World Health Organization, accessed November 15, 2022, https://www.who.int/emergencies/situations/ukraine-emergency/technological-hazards-and-health-risks-in-ukraine.

16. "War Sets Back the Global Recovery," International Monetary Fund, April 19, 2022, https://www.imf.org/en/Publications/WEO/Issues/2022/04/19/world-economic-outlook-april-2022.

17. Katherine Schaeffer, "A Growing Share of Americans Say Affordable Housing Is a Major Problem Where They Live," Pew Research Center, January 18, 2022, https://www.pewresearch.org/fact-tank/2022/01/18/a-growing-share-of-americans-say-affordable-housing-is-a-major-problem-where-they-live/.

18. Jeroen Wolbers, Sanneke Kuipers, and Arjen Boin, "A Systematic Review of 20 Years of Crisis and Disaster Research: Trends and Progress," *Risk, Hazards & Crisis in Public Policy* 12, no. 4 (2021): 374–392, https://onlinelibrary.wiley.com/doi/full/10.1002/rhc3.12244.

19. Fikret Berkes and Helen Ross, "Community Resilience: Toward an Integrated Approach," *Society & Natural Resources* 26, no. 1 (2013): 5–20, https://www.tandfonline.com/doi/abs/10.1080/08941920.2012.736605?journalCode=usnr20.

20. Arjen Boin, Magnus Ekengren, and Mark Rhinard, "Hiding in Plain Sight: Conceptualizing the Creeping Crisis," *Risk, Hazards & Crisis in Public Policy* 11, no. 2 (2020): 116–138, https://onlinelibrary.wiley.com/doi/full/10.1002/rhc3.12193.

21. Sarah Fitzpatrick, "Why the Strategic National Stockpile Isn't Meant to Solve a Crisis Like Coronavirus," *NBC News*, March 28, 2020, https://www.nbcnews.com/health/health-care/why-strategic-national-stockpile-isn-t-meant-solve-crisis-coronavirus-n1170376.

22. Betsy McKay and Phred Dvorak, "A Deadly Coronavirus Was Inevitable. Why Was No One Ready?," *The Wall Street Journal*, August 13, https://www.wsj.com/articles/a-deadly-coronavirus-was-inevitable-why-was-no-one-ready-for-covid-11597325213 2020.

23. Jeroen Wolbers, Sanneke Kuipers, and Arjen Boin, "A Systematic Review of 20 Years of Crisis and Disaster Research: Trends and Progress," *Risk, Hazards, & Crisis in Public Policy* 12 (2021): 374–392, https://doi.org/10.1002/rhc3.12244.

24. Bryan Strawser, "Beyond ROI: The Value of Effective Crisis Management," Bryghtpath, September 20, 2022, https://bryghtpath.com/beyond-roi-the-value-of-effective-crisis-management/.

25. Meng Zhao, Seung Ho Park, and Nan Zhou, "MNC Strategy and Social Adaptation in Emerging Markets," *Journal of International Business Studies*, 45, no. 7 (2014): 842–861, https://link.springer.com/article/10.1057/jibs.2014.8.

26. Eric McNulty et al., "Leading through Covid-19: A Meta-Leadership Analysis," National Preparedness Leadership Initiative, accessed November 15, 2022, https://cdn1.sph.harvard.edu/wp-content/uploads/sites/2443/2021/12/NPLI-DRI-Covid-Lessons-Report-12-14-2021.pdf.

27. Chris Argyris, "Teaching Smart People How to Learn," *Harvard Business Review*, June 1, 1991, https://hbr.org/1991/05/teaching-smart-people-how-to-learn.

28. Bryan Lufkin, "Why Presenteeism Wins Out over Productivity," *BBC Worklife*, June 7, 2021, https://www.bbc.com/worklife/article/20210604-why-presenteeism-always-wins-out-over-productivity.

29. "Priorities for the C-Suite in 2022," BCG, January 10, 2022, https://www.bcg.com/publications/2022/c-suite-executive-priorities-2022#gilbert.

30. Timothy W. Coombs and Daniel Laufer, *Global Crisis Management*, 199–203.

31. Kelly M. Davis and William L. Gardner, "Charisma Under Crisis Revisited: Presidential Leadership, Perceived Leader Effectiveness, and Contextual Influences," *The Leadership Quarterly*, 23, no. 5 (2012): 918–933, https://www.sciencedirect.com/science/article/pii/S1048984312000483.

32. Pillai Rajnandini and James R. Meindl, "Context and Charisma: A 'Meso' Level Examination of the Relationship of Organic Structure, Collectivism, and Crisis to Charismatic Leadership," *Journal of Management* 24, no. 5 (1998): 643–671, https://www.sciencedirect.com/science/article/abs/pii/S0149206399800786.

33. Jonathan Rothwell and Christos Makridis, "Politics Is Wrecking America's Pandemic Response," Brookings, September 17, 2020, https://www.brookings.edu/blog/up-front/2020/09/17/politics-is-wrecking-americas-pandemic-response/.

34. Markus Hällgren, Linda Rouleau, and Mark De Rond, "A Matter of Life or Death: How Extreme Context Research Matters for Management and Organization Studies," *Academy of Management Annals* 12, no. 1 (2018): 111–153, https://journals.aom.org/doi/abs/10.5465/annals.2016.0017.

35. "Stress in America: Money, Inflation, War Pile on to Nation Stuck in COVID-19 Survival Mode," American Psychological Association, March 11, 2022, https://www.apa.org/news/press/releases/stress/2022/march-2022-survival-mode.

36. Chris Ansell, Arjen Boin, and Ann Keller, "Managing Transboundary Crises: Identifying the Building Blocks of an Effective Response System," *Journal of Contingencies and Crisis Management* 18, no. 4 (2010): 195-207, https://onlinelibrary.wiley.com/doi/abs/10.1111/j.1468-5973.2010.00620.x.

37. Arjen Boin, "The Transboundary Crisis: Why We Are Unprepared and the Road Ahead," *Journal of Contingencies and Crisis Management* 27, no. 1 (2019): 94–99, https://onlinelibrary.wiley.com/doi/full/10.1111/1468-5973.12241.

38. Enrico L. Quarantelli, "Disaster Studies: The Consequences of the Historical Use of a Sociological Approach in the Development of Research," *International Journal of Mass Emergencies and Disasters* 12, no. 1 (1994): 25–49, https://www.safetylit.org/citations/index.php?fuseaction=citations.viewdetails&citationIds[]=citjournalarticle_56054_12.

39. Jeroen Wolbers, Sanneke Kuipers, and Arjen Boin, "A Systematic Review of 20 Years of Crisis and Disaster Research: Trends and Progress," *Risk, Hazards, & Crisis in Public Policy*, 12 (2021): 374–392, https://doi.org/10.1002/rhc3.12244.

40. "Why Giving Is Good for Your Health," Cleveland Clinic, October 28, 2020, https://health.clevelandclinic.org/why-giving-is-good-for-your-health/.

41. "Global Flood Awareness System," European Commission, accessed November 15, 2022, https://www.globalfloods.eu/.

42. Tarek Ghani and Grant Gordon, "Predictable Disasters: AI and the Future of Crisis Response," in *Breakthrough: The Promise of Frontier Technologies for Sustainable Development*, ed. by Homi Kharas, John W. McArthur, Izumi Ohno (Washington, DC: The Brooking Institute, 2022): 103–124, https://www.brookings.edu/wp-content/uploads/2021/12/Chapter-Six_Breakthrough.pdf.

43. "Behavioral Finance & Financial Stability," Harvard Business School, accessed November 15, 2022, https://www.hbs.edu/behavioral-finance-and-financial-stability/data/Pages/global.aspx.

44. Aristeidis Samitas, Elias Kampouris, and Dimitris Kenourgios, "Machine Learning as an Early Warning System to Predict Financial Crisis," *International Review of Financial Analysis* 71 (2020): 101507, https://www.sciencedirect.com/science/article/abs/pii/S1057521920301514.

45. Alexander S. Gillis, "What Is the Internet of Things (IoT)?" TechTarget, March 4, 2022, https://www.techtarget.com/iotagenda/definition/Internet-of-Things-IoT.

46. Wil M.P. van der Aalst, "Process Mining: A 360 Degree Overview," in *Process Mining Handbook*, ed. by Wil M.P. van der Aalst and Josep Carmona (Cham: Springer, 2022), 3–34, https://link.springer.com/chapter/10.1007/978-3-031-08848-3_1.

47. "Tony's Beantracker," Tony's Chocolonley, accessed November 15, 2022, https://tonyschocolonely.com/nl/en/our-mission/serious-statements/tonys-beantracker.

48. P. Arun Mozhi Devan et al., "IoT Based Water Usage Monitoring System Using LabVIEW," in *Smart Technologies and Innovation for a Sustainable Future*, ed. by Ahmed Al-Masri and Kevin Curran (Cham: Springer, 2019), 205–212, https://link.springer.com/chapter/10.1007/978-3-030-01659-3_23.

49. Martin Macak et al., "Process Mining Usage in Cybersecurity and Software Reliability Analysis: A Systematic Literature Review," *Array* (2021): 100120, https://www.sciencedirect.com/science/article/pii/S2590005621000576.

50. Michael Becker and Rüdiger Buchkremer, "A Practical Process Mining Approach for Compliance Management," *Journal of Financial Regulation and Compliance* 27 (2019), 464–478, https://www.emerald.com/insight/content/doi/10.1108/JFRC-12-2018-0163/full/html.

51. "CrisisWatch," International Crisis Group, accessed November 15, 2022, https://www.crisisgroup.org/crisiswatch.

52. "COVID-19 Dashboard," John Hopkins Coronavirus Resource Center, accessed November 15, 2022, https://coronavirus.jhu.edu/map.html.

53. Corinne Purtill, "This COVID-19 Tracker Changed How We Saw the Pandemic: Its Creator Fears It Won't Be Useful Much Longer," *Los Angeles Times*, September 28, 2022, https://www.latimes.com/science/story/2022-09-28/lauren-gardner-wins-lasker-award-for-johns-hopkins-covid-19-dashboard.

54. "COVID-19 Global Gender Response Tracker," United Nations Development Programme, accessed November 15, 2022, https://data.undp.org/gendertracker/.

55. Marieke van Gompel, "How a Communications Failure Crippled the Dutch Rail Network," RailTech, June, 02, 2021, https://www.railtech.

com/infrastructure/2021/06/02/how-a-communications-failure-crippled-the-dutch-rail-network/?gdpr=deny.

56. Stanimira Ruseva, "Understanding Public Sentiment for Public Safety & Security," PublicSonar, June 15, 2021, https://publicsonar.com/understanding-public-sentiment-for-public-safety-security/.

57. "10 Ways You Can Relieve Stress Right Now," Cleveland Clinic, May 26, 2022, https://health.clevelandclinic.org/how-to-relieve-stress/.

58. Stefan Seidel et al., "Autonomous Tools and Design: A Triple-Loop Approach to Human-Machine Learning," *Communications of the ACM* 62, no. 1 (2018): 50–57.

59. "Future of Work Trends 2022: A New Era of Humanity," Korn Ferry (2021), https://www.kornferry.com/content/dam/kornferry-v2/featured-topics/pdf/FOW_TrendsReport_2022.pdf.

60. "Nasdaq Launches Artificial Intelligence for Surveillance Patterns on U.S. Stock Market," Nasdaq, November 7, 2019, https://www.nasdaq.com/press-release/nasdaq-launches-artificial-intelligence-for-surveillance-patterns-on-u.s.-stock.

61. Akash Gupta and Amir Gharehgozli, "Developing a Machine Learning Framework to Determine the Spread of COVID-19 in the USA Using Meteorological, Social, and Demographic Factors," *International Journal of Data Mining, Modelling and Management* 14, no. 2 (2022): 89–109, https://www.inderscienceonline.com/doi/abs/10.1504/IJDMMM.2022.123360.

62. Yongjiu Feng et al., "Spatiotemporal Spread Pattern of the COVID-19 Cases in China." *PLOS ONE* 15, no. 12 (2020): e0244351, https://journals.plos.org/plosone/article?id=10.1371/journal.pone.0244351.

63. Ania Syrowatka et al., "Leveraging Artificial Intelligence for Pandemic Preparedness and Response: A Scoping Review to Identify Key Use Cases," *NPJ Digital Medicine* 4, no. 1 (2021): 1–14, https://www.nature.com/articles/s41746-021-00459-8.

Chapter 6: Cultivating Healthy Growth with Healthy People

1. Kaysie Brown, "5 Global Issues to Watch in 2022," United Nations Foundation, December 21, 2021, https://unfoundation.org/blog/post/5-global-issues-to-watch-in-2022/.

2. "The Triple Billion Targets: A Visual Summary of Methods to Deliver Impact," World Health Organization, accessed November 15, 2022,

https://www.who.int/data/stories/the-triple-billion-targets-a-visual-summary-of-methods-to-deliver-impact.

3. "Triple Billion Dashboard," World Health Organization, accessed November 15, 2022, https://portal.who.int/triplebillions/.

4. Salinatri, "G20 Joint Finance and Health Minister Meeting Concludes the Year to Affirm Commitment to Strengthen Global Health Architecture," G20, November 13, 2022, https://www.g20.org/g20-joint-finance-and-health-minister-meeting-concludes-the-year-to-affirm-commitment-to-strengthen-global-health-architecture/.

5. Grant Robertson, "Budget 2022 to Boost Health and Climate Action," New Zealand Government, December 15, 2021, https://www.beehive.govt.nz/release/budget-2022-boost-health-and-climate-action.

6. Joyce Teo, "Budget 2022: Healthcare Spending to Form Bulk of Increase in Social Expenditures by 2030," *The Straits Times*, February 18, 2022, https://www.straitstimes.com/singapore/budget-2022-healthcare-spending-to-form-bulk-of-govt-expenditure-by-2030.

7. "Strong Public Health Care," Government of Canada, April 7, 2022, https://www.budget.gc.ca/2022/report-rapport/chap6-en.html.

8. "Our Priorities for 2021/2022," HM Government, March 30, 2021, https://communication-plan.gcs.civilservice.gov.uk/our-priorities/.

9. "The Biden-Harris Administration Immediate Priorities," The White House, September 20, 2021, https://www.whitehouse.gov/priorities/.

10. "2022 Voice of the Superintendent Survey," EAB, accessed November 15, 2022, https://ml.globenewswire.com/Resource/Download/f2018b5d-a9d9-4fb3-96c3-167c92c3cd92.

11. "Preparing for a COVID-19-Safe Ramadan in 2022: A Virtual Panel Discussion with Religious Scholars," World Health Organization, March 20, 2022, https://www.emro.who.int/media/news/preparing-for-a-covid-19-safe-ramadan-in-2022-a-virtual-panel-discussion-with-religious-scholars.html.

12. Gary Claxton et al., "How Corporate Executives View Rising Health Care Cost and the Role of Government," Kaiser Family Foundation, April 29, 2021, https://www.kff.org/health-reform/report/how-large-employers-view-rising-health-care-cost-and-the-role-of-government/.

13. "AI for Social Good," Google, accessed November 15, 2022, https://ai.google/social-good/.

14. "Data for Good at Meta," Meta, accessed November 15, 2022, https://dataforgood.facebook.com/dfg/about.

15. "AI for Good," Microsoft, accessed November 15, 2022, https://www.microsoft.com/en-us/ai/ai-for-good.

16. "What Are Paramedical Services? Everything You Need to Know," Olympia Benefits, June 2, 2021, https://www.olympiabenefits.com/blog/what-are-paramedical-services.

17. "Build Your People's Mental Resilience," Stanford Medicine and Thrive Global, accessed November 15, 2022, https://info.thriveglobal.com/solutions-thriving-mind.htm.

18. Francisco Ortega and Michael Orsini, "Governing COVID-19 without Government in Brazil: Ignorance, Neoliberal Authoritarianism, and the Collapse of Public Health Leadership," *Global Public Health* 15, no. 9 (2020): 1257–1277, https://www.tandfonline.com/doi/full/10.1080/17441692.2020.1795223.

19. "Considering Digital Mental Health Tools for Your Employees," American Psychological Association, April 27, 2022, https://www.apa.org/topics/workplace/digital-mental-health-tools.

20. "About Global NCDs," Centers for Disease Control and Prevention, accessed November 15, 2022, https://www.cdc.gov/globalhealth/health-protection/ncd/global-ncd-overview.html.

21. "Billions of People Still Breathe Unhealthy Air: New WHO Data," World Health Organization, April 4, 2022, https://www.who.int/news/item/04-04-2022-billions-of-people-still-breathe-unhealthy-air-new-who-data.

22. Howard J. Bolnick et al., "Health-Care Spending Attributable to Modifiable Risk Factors in the USA: An Economic Attribution Analysis," *The Lancet Public Health* 5, no. 10 (2020): e525–e535, https://www.thelancet.com/journals/lanpub/article/PIIS2468-2667(20)30203-6/fulltext.

23. Sandro Galea and Nason Maani, "The Cost of Preventable Disease in the USA," *The Lancet Public Health* 5, no. 10 (2020): e513–e514, https://www.thelancet.com/journals/lanpub/article/PIIS2468-2667(20)30204-8/fulltext.

24. "World Health Statistics 2022," World Health Organization, May 20, 2022, https://www.who.int/news/item/20-05-2022-world-health-statistics-2022.

25. "Employer Costs for Employee Compensation: June 2022," U.S. Bureau of Labor Statistics, September 20, 2022, https://www.bls.gov/news.release/pdf/ecec.pdf.

26. Gary Claxton et al., "How Corporate Executives View Rising Health Care Cost and the Role of Government," Kaiser Family Foundation, April 29, 2021, https://www.kff.org/health-reform/report/how-large-employers-view-rising-health-care-cost-and-the-role-of-government/.

27. John Delmatoff and Ian R. Lazarus, "The Most Effective Leadership Style for the New Landscape of Healthcare," *Journal of Healthcare*

Management 59, no. 4 (2014): 245–249, https://journals.lww.com/jhmon-line/Fulltext/2014/07000/The_Most_Effective_Leadership_Style_for_the_New.3.aspx.

28. Marta Roczniewska et al., "Beyond the Individual: A Systematic Review of the Effects of Unit-Level Demands and Resources on Employee Productivity, Health, and Well-Being," *Journal of Occupational Health Psychology* 27, no. 2 (2022): 240, https://psycnet.apa.org/fulltext/2022-04886-001.html.

29. Tor Ingebrigtsen et al., "The Impact of Clinical Leadership on Health Information Technology Adoption: Systematic Review," *International Journal of Medical Informatics* 83, no. 6 (2014): 393–405, https://www.sciencedirect.com/science/article/abs/pii/S1386505614000446.

30. Brian R. Spisak, "How Data Can Make Better Managers," *Harvard Business Review*, March 2, 2022, https://hbr.org/2022/03/how-data-can-make-better-managers.

31. "Employer Solutions: Better Care. Better Outcomes. Better Value," Cleveland Clinic, accessed November 15, 2022, https://my.cleveland-clinic.org/departments/employer-healthcare-solutions.

32. Tor Ingebrigtsen et al., "The Impact of Clinical Leadership on Health Information Technology Adoption: Systematic Review," 393–405.

33. Tor Ingebrigtsen et al., "The Impact of Clinical Leadership on Health Information Technology Adoption: Systematic Review," 398.

34. Nizar Bhulani et al., "Leadership in Healthcare: A Bibliometric Analysis of 100 Most Influential Publications," *BMJ Leader* 5 (2020): 65–68, https://bmjleader.bmj.com/content/5/1/65.info.

35. Robert H. Shmerling, "Is Our Healthcare System Broken?," *Harvard Health Publishing*, July 13, 2021, https://www.health.harvard.edu/blog/is-our-healthcare-system-broken-202107132542.

36. Nizar Bhulani et al., "Leadership in Healthcare: A Bibliometric Analysis of 100 Most Influential Publications," 65–68.

37. "Empowering Leaders to Lead Change," American Association for Physician Leadership, accessed November 15, 2022, https://www.physicianleaders.org/.

38. "ASA-CPLE Leader Focus Assessment," American Society of Anesthesiologists Center for Physician Leadership Excellence, accessed November 15, 2022, https://www.asahq.org/education-and-career/leadership development/cple.

39. "Cultivating Leadership Measure and Assess Leader Behaviors to Improve Professional Well-Being," American Medical Association, accessed November 15, 2022, https://edhub.ama-assn.org/steps-forward/module/2774089.

40. John Hagel, *The Journey Beyond Fear: Leverage the Three Pillars of Positivity to Build Your Success* (New York: McGraw Hill, 2021), https://www.mhprofessional.com/the-journey-beyond-fear-leverage-the-three-pillars-of-positivity-to-build-your-success-9781264268405-usa.

41. American Medical Association, *Cultivating Leadership*, accessed November 15, 2022; American Association for Physician Leadership, *Empowering Leaders*, accessed November 15, 2022; American Society of Anesthesiologists Center for Physician Leadership Excellence, *ASA-CPLE Leader Focus*, accessed November 15, 2022; Hogan Assessments, accessed November 15, 2022, https://www.hoganassessments.com/.

42. "Big 5 Personality Traits," *Psychology Today*, November 22, 2017, https://www.psychologytoday.com/us/basics/big-5-personality-traits.

43. Vincent Q. Sier et al., "Exploring the Surgical Personality," *The Surgeon* (2022), https://doi.org/10.1016/j.surge.2022.01.008.

44. Justin Barad, "Virtual and Augmented Reality Can Save Lives by Improving Surgeons' Training," *STAT*, August 16, 2019, https://www.statnews.com/2019/08/16/virtual-reality-improve-surgeon-training/.

45. Jay Croft, "Virtual Reality Fitness? 'Yeah, It's a Workout,'" WebMD, February 23, 2022, https://www.webmd.com/fitness-exercise/news/20220223/virtual-reality-fitness-a-workout.

46. Paul M.G. Emmelkamp and Katharina Meyerbröker, "Virtual Reality Therapy in Mental Health," *Annual Review of Clinical Psychology* 17 (2021): 495–519, https://www.annualreviews.org/doi/abs/10.1146/annurev-clinpsy-081219-115923.

47. Brennan Spiegel et al., "Virtual Reality for Management of Pain in Hospitalized Patients: A Randomized Comparative Effectiveness Trial," *PLOS ONE* 14, no. 8 (2019): e0219115, https://journals.plos.org/plosone/article?id=10.1371/journal.pone.0219115.

48. Rutwik Shah et al., "Utilizing a Digital Swarm Intelligence Platform to Improve Consensus Among Radiologists and Exploring Its Applications," *arXiv preprint arXiv:2107.07341* (2021), https://arxiv.org/abs/2107.07341.

49. "What Is Interoperability in Healthcare?," IBM, accessed November 15, 2022, https://www.ibm.com/topics/interoperability-in-healthcare.

50. UneeQ, accessed November 15, 2022, https://digitalhumans.com/.

51. Gianni Giacomelli, "Augmented Collective Intelligence: Human-AI Networks in a Virtual Future of Work, and How They Change Our World," *Medium*, November 2, 2021, https://medium.com/@giannigiacomelli69/augmented-collective-intelligence-22ad9561f557.

Chapter 7: Becoming a Digital Golf Pro and Growing Digital Trees

1. Brian R. Spisak, "How Data Can Make Better Managers," *Harvard Business Review*, March 2, 2022, https://hbr.org/2022/03/how-data-can-make-better-managers.
2. Rebecca Knight, "7 Practical Ways to Reduce Bias in Your Hiring Process," *Harvard Business Review*, June 12, 2017, https://hbr.org/2017/06/7-practical-ways-to-reduce-bias-in-your-hiring-process.
3. "The Cognitive Bias Codex," accessed November 17, 2022, https://commons.wikimedia.org/wiki/File:Cognitive_bias_codex_en.svg.
4. Ruchika Tulshyan, "How to Reduce Personal Bias When Hiring," *Harvard Business Review*, June 28, 2019, https://hbr.org/2019/06/how-to-reduce-personal-bias-when-hiring.
5. Bomin Jiang, Daniel Rigobon, and Roberto Rigobon, "From Just-in-Time, to Just-in-Case, to Just-in-Worst-Case: Simple Models of a Global Supply Chain under Uncertain Aggregate Shocks," *IMF Economic Review* 70, no. 1 (2022): 141–184, https://doi.org/10.1057/s41308-021-00148-2.
6. Xing Xie et al., "Personalized Recommendation Systems: Five Hot Research Topics You Must Know," Microsoft Research Lab: Asia (2018), https://www.microsoft.com/en-us/research/lab/microsoft-research-asia/articles/personalized-recommendation-systems/.
7. Thomson Reuters, "Thomson Reuters Launches First of its Kind Knowledge Graph Feed Allowing Financial Services Customers to Accelerate their AI and Digital Strategies," news release, October 23, 2017, https://www.thomsonreuters.com/en/press-releases/2017/october/thomson-reuters-launches-first-of-its-kind-knowledge-graph-feed.html.
8. Brian R. Spisak, "Tinbergen's Take on the Evolution of Leadership: A Framework for Clarifying and Integrating Contributions," *The Leadership Quarterly* 31, no. 2 (2020): e101401, https://doi.org/10.1016/j.leaqua.2020.101401.
9. Ken Kocienda, *Creative Selection: Inside Apple's Design Process During the Golden Age of Steve Jobs* (London: Pan Macmillan, 2018).
10. "Delta Chooses EpiAnalytics® TextBI to Analyze Employee Sentiment on Workplace from Facebook During COVID-19," J.D. Power, accessed November 17, 2022, https://www.jdpower.com/sites/default/files/file/2021-07/EpiAnalytics_Workplace%2BFacebook_Case_Study_FINAL.pdf.
11. "Diversity, Equity and Inclusion: Fostering DE&I in Our Organization and Yours," Automatic Data Processing Inc., accessed November 17, 2022, https://www.adp.com/resources/diversity-equity-and-inclusion.aspx.

12. "Diversity Dashboard," Massachusetts Institute of Technology, accessed November 17, 2022, https://ir.mit.edu/diversity-dashboard.

13. Kevin Martin, "How Cisco Uses a Data-Driven Approach to Strategic Workforce Planning," *i4cp*, May 16, 2020, https://www.i4cp.com/interviews/how-cisco-uses-a-data-driven-approach-to-strategic-workforce-planning?search_id=302295.

14. Kenneth E. Boulding, "General Systems Theory: The Skeleton of Science," *Management Science* 2, no. 3 (1956): 207, https://doi.org/10.1287/mnsc.2.3.197.

15. Jackie Wiles, "Workforce Issues Loom Large, While Sustainability Becomes a Mainstream Concern," Gartner, April 27, 2022, https://www.gartner.com/en/articles/ceos-turn-a-sharp-eye-to-workforce-issues-and-sustainability-in-2022-23.

16. Venky Anant, Jeffrey Caso, and Andreas Schwarz, "COVID-19 Crisis Shifts Cybersecurity Priorities and Budgets," McKinsey & Company, July 21, 2020, https://www.mckinsey.com/capabilities/risk-and-resilience/our-insights/covid-19-crisis-shifts-cybersecurity-priorities-and-budgets.

17. Faheem Gul Gilal et al., "The Role of Self-Determination Theory in Marketing Science: An Integrative Review and Agenda for Research," *European Management Journal* 37, no. 1 (2019): 29–44, https://doi.org/10.1016/j.emj.2018.10.004.

18. Gerald C. Kane et al., "Teaming Your Way Through Disruption," *Deloitte Insights*, October 26, 2021, https://www2.deloitte.com/uk/en/insights/topics/strategy/cross-functional-collaboration.html.

19. Richard M. Ryan and Edward L. Deci, "Self-Determination Theory and the Facilitation of Intrinsic Motivation, Social Development, and Well-Being," *American Psychologist* 55, no. 1 (2000): 68–78, https://doi.org/10.1037/0003-066X.55.1.68.

20. James G. March, "Exploration and Exploitation in Organizational Learning," *Organization Science* 2, no. 1 (1991): 71–87, https://doi.org/10.1287/orsc.2.1.71.

21. Liz Mineo, "Good Genes Are Nice, but Joy Is Better," *The Harvard Gazette*, April 11, 2017, https://news.harvard.edu/gazette/story/2017/04/over-nearly-80-years-harvard-study-has-been-showing-how-to-live-a-healthy-and-happy-life/.

22. Laura Albert, "Anytime, Anywhere HR: How Mobile is Key to Connecting the Disconnected," *Forbes*, June 30, 2021, https://www.forbes.com/sites/sap/2021/06/30/anytime-anywhere-hr-how-mobile-is-key-to-connecting-the-disconnected.

23. Julie Cook Ramirez, "These New Technologies are Transforming Mentoring Programs," *Human Resource Executive*, January 9, 2019, https://

hrexecutive.com/these-new-technologies-are-transforming-mentoring-programs/.

24. Eric J. McNulty, "Leading in an Increasingly VUCA World," strategy+business, October 27, 2015, https://www.strategy-business.com/blog/Leading-in-an-Increasingly-VUCA-World.

25. Kon Leong, "A Data-Driven Approach to Identifying—and Retaining—Top Employees," *Harvard Business Review*, May, 14, 2021, https://hbr.org/2021/05/a-data-driven-approach-to-identifying-and-retaining-top-employees.

26. Vijay Arya et al., "One Explanation Does Not Fit All: A Toolkit and Taxonomy of AI Explainability Techniques," *arXiv preprint arXiv: 1909.03012* (2019), https://doi.org/10.48550/arXiv.1909.03012.

27. Tomas Chamorro-Premuzic, Seymour Adler, and Robert B. Kaiser, "What Science Says about Identifying High-Potential Employees," *Harvard Business Review*, October 3, 2017, https://hbr.org/2017/10/what-science-says-about-identifying-high-potential-employees.

28. Randstad, "Tap Into Collective Intelligence for Better Hiring Outcomes," June 8, 2020, https://www.randstad.com/workforce-insights/hr-tech/tap-collective-intelligence-better-hiring-outcomes.

29. Catherine Cote, "What Is Predictive Analytics? 5 Examples," *Harvard Business School Online*, October 26, 2021, https://online.hbs.edu/blog/post/predictive-analytics.

30. N Llort et al., "A Decision Support System and a Mathematical Model for Strategic Workforce Planning in Consultancies," *Flexible Services and Manufacturing Journal* 31, no. 2 (2019): 497–523, https://doi.org/10.1007/s10696-018-9321-2.

31. Shilpa Pai Mizar, "Using Predictive Analytics in Employee Retention: This Technique Can Help Managers Reduce Attrition Costs," *Financial Management*, December 1, 2018, https://www.fm-magazine.com/issues/2018/dec/using-predictive-analytics-in-employee-retention.html.

32. HSC Analytics, accessed November 17, 2022, https://www.hscanalytics.com/.

33. "Digital Human: Elevating the Digital Human Experience," Deloitte, accessed November 17, 2022, https://www2.deloitte.com/nl/nl/pages/customer-and-marketing/articles/digital-human.html#.

34. Jeff Koyen, "The Pitfalls of Subpar Knowledge Sharing Systems: A Conversation with Stack Overflow's Vasudha Swaminathan," *Forbes*, July 16, 2021, https://www.forbes.com/sites/stack-overflow-for-teams/2021/07/16/the-pitfalls-of-subpar-knowledge-sharing-systems-a-conversation-with-stack-overflows-vasudha-swaminathan.

35. "Data Fabric: The Transformative Next Step in Data Management," Informatica, accessed November 17, 2022, https://www.informatica.com/nl/resources/articles/data-fabric-the-transformative-next-step-in-data-management.html.
36. Malcolm Murray and Laura Reul, "Why Dynamic Risk Governance Starts with Shared Data," Gartner, May 6, 2022, https://www.gartner.com/en/articles/why-dynamic-risk-governance-starts-with-shared-data.

CHAPTER 8: NAVIGATING THE 4 Cs OF DIGITAL TRANSFORMATION

1. Satish Nambisan and Priya Nambisan, "Engaging Citizens in Co-Creation in Public Services," *IBM Center for Business Development* (2013): 8–48, https://www.businessofgovernment.org/sites/default/files/Engaging%20Citizens%20in%20Co-Creation%20in%20Public%20Service.pdf.
2. Graeme Nicholas et al., "Towards a Heart and Soul for Co-Creative Research Practice: A Systemic Approach," *Evidence & Policy* 15, no. 3 (2019): 353–370, https://doi.org/10.1332/174426419X15578220630571.
3. Aaron De Smet, Gerald Lackey, and Leigh M. Weiss, "Untangling Your Organization's Decision Making," McKinsey & Company, June 21, 2017, https://www.mckinsey.com/capabilities/people-and-organizational-performance/our-insights/untangling-your-organizations-decision-making.
4. Daniel Kahneman, Dan Lovallo, and Olivier Sibony, "Before You Make that Big Decision," *Harvard Business Review* 89, no. 6 (2011): 50–60, https://hbr.org/2011/06/the-big-idea-before-you-make-that-big-decision.
5. "Recent Study Reveals More Than a Third of Global Consumers Are Willing to Pay More for Sustainability as Demand Grows for Environmentally-Friendly Alternatives," Simon-Kucher & Partners, October 25, 2021, https://www.simon-kucher.com/en/about/media-center/recent-study-reveals-more-third-global-consumers-are-willing-pay-more-sustainability-demand-grows-environmentally-friendly-alternatives.
6. Björn Hofman, Gerdien de Vries, and Geerten van de Kaa, "Keeping Things as They Are: How Status Quo Biases and Traditions along with a Lack of Information Transparency in the Building Industry Slow Down the Adoption of Innovative Sustainable Technologies," *Sustainability* 14, no. 13 (2022): 8188, https://doi.org/10.3390/su14138188.
7. Tara Van Bommel, "Remote-Work Options Can Boost Productivity and Curb Burnout (Report)," Catalyst (2021), https://www.catalyst.org/reports/remote-work-burnout-productivity/.

8. Debora Jeske, "Monitoring Remote Employees: Implications for HR," *Strategic HR Review* 20, no. 2 (2021): 42–46, https://doi.org/10.1108/SHR-10-2020-0089.

9. Jackie Wiles, "CEOs Turn a Sharp Eye to Workforce Issues and Sustainability in 2022–23," Gartner, April 27, 2022, https://www.gartner.com/en/articles/ceos-turn-a-sharp-eye-to-workforce-issues-and-sustainability-in-2022-23.

10. "Deloitte Survey: Analytics and Data-driven Culture Help Companies Outperform Business Goals in the 'Age of With,'" Deloitte, July 25, 2019, https://www2.deloitte.com/us/en/pages/about-deloitte/articles/press-releases/deloitte-survey-analytics-and-ai-driven-enterprises-thrive.html.

11. "Tony's Beantracker," Tony's Chocolonely, accessed November 19, 2022, https://tonyschocolonely.com/nl/en/our-mission/serious-statements/tonys-beantracker.

12. Ryan Kaiser, David Schatsky, and Robin Jones, "Collaboration at a Distance: Technology for Remote, High-Touch Scenarios," Deloitte, October 28, 2020, https://www2.deloitte.com/us/en/insights/focus/signals-for-strategists/virtual-team-collaboration.html.

13. Robert Lee, "Social Capital and Business and Management: Setting a Research Agenda," *International Journal of Management Reviews* 11, no. 3 (2009): 247–273, https://doi.org/10.1111/j.1468-2370.2008.00244.x.

14. Brian R. Spisak et al., "Niche Construction and the Evolution of Leadership," *Academy of Management Review* 40, no. 2 (2015): 291–306, https://doi.org/10.5465/amr.2013.0157.

15. Kristin L. Cullen, Charles J. Palus, and Craig Appaneal, "Developing Network Perspective Understanding the Basics of Social Networks and their Role in Leadership," *Center for Creative Leadership*, accessed November 19, 2022, https://www.cclinsights.com/MediaServer/118/documents/DevelopingNetworkPerspective.pdf.

16. Stephen Moore, "Porsche in Joint Effort for Plastics Traceability," Plastics Today, November 10, 2020, https://www.plasticstoday.com/sustainability/porsche-joint-effort-plastics-traceability.

17. George T. Doran, "There's a SMART Way to Write Management's Goals and Objectives," *Management Review* 70, no. 11 (1981): 35–36, https://community.mis.temple.edu/mis0855002fall2015/files/2015/10/S.M.A.R.T-Way-Management-Review.pdf.

18. Andrew Allen, "Supplier's CO2 Emissions will be Part of Tender Process, Says BMW," Supply Management, July 29, 2020, https://www.cips.org/supply-management/news/2020/july/suppliers-co2-emissions-will-be-part-of-tender-process-says-bmw/.

19. Larry Fink, "2022 Letter to CEOS: The Power of Capitalism," BlackRock, accessed November 18, 2022, https://www.blackrock.com/corporate/investor-relations/larry-fink-ceo-letter.

20. Mickael Brossard, "Digital Twins: The Art of the Possible in Product Development and Beyond," McKinsey & Company, April 28, 2022, https://www.mckinsey.com/capabilities/operations/our-insights/digital-twins-the-art-of-the-possible-in-product-development-and-beyond.

21. "Gartner Forecasts Worldwide IT Spending to Reach $4.4 Trillion in 2022," Gartner, April 6, 2022, https://www.gartner.com/en/newsroom/press-releases/2022-04-06-gartner-forecasts-worldwide-it-spending-to-reach-4-point-four-trillion-in-2022.

22. William Touche, Dan Konigsburg, and Jo Iwasaki, "Digital Frontier: A Technology Deficit in the Boardroom," Deloitte, June 13, 2022, https://www2.deloitte.com/us/en/insights/topics/leadership/digital-transformation-topics-for-corporate-technology-leadership.html.

Conclusion: Spider-Man and Your Post-Digital Future

1. Sonya Dineva, "Convincing Your Company Leaders to Invest in New Technology," *Harvard Business Review*, January 18, 2022, https://hbr.org/2022/01/convincing-your-company-leaders-to-invest-in-new-technology.

2. "Coming Soon to Your Business: Quantum Computing," IBM, November 1, 2018, https://www.ibm.com/thought-leadership/institute-business-value/report/quantumstrategy.

3. Andreas Trabesinger, "Quantum Simulation," *Nature Physics* 8, no. 4 (2012): 263–263, https://doi.org/10.1038/nphys2258.

4. Alvaro Huerga et al., "A Quantum Computing Approach to Human Behavior Prediction," *2022 7th International Conference on Smart and Sustainable Technologies (SpliTech)*, 1–5, IEEE, 2022, https://doi.org/10.23919/SpliTech55088.2022.9854257.

5. Javier Villalba-Diez et al., "Industry 4.0 Quantum Strategic Organizational Design Configurations. The Case of 3 Qubits: One Reports to Two," *Entropy* 23, no. 3 (2021): 374, https://doi.org/10.3390/e23030374.

6. "Digital Human: Elevating the Digital Human Experience," Deloitte, February 23, 2021, https://www2.deloitte.com/nl/nl/pages/customer-and-marketing/articles/digital-human.html.

7. "Facts and Figures 2021: 2.9 Billion People Still Offline," UN International Telecommunication Union, November 29, 2021, https://www.itu.int/hub/2021/11/facts-and-figures-2021-2-9-billion-people-still-offline/.

ACKNOWLEDGMENTS

First and foremost, I would like to thank my wife, Nancy, for her patience and support throughout this process. You're always in my corner, and I'm forever grateful! My appreciation to all of my friends and family for always believing in me. I also extend many thanks to the leaders who participated in the Q&As: Sofia Lamuraglia and Jennifer Sevilla Montana at IBM, Cecil Peters at JPMorgan Chase, Lauren Boyatzi at Merck, Paul Schoenmakers at Tony's Chocolonely, Jennie Clinton at Microsoft, and John Whyte at WebMD. And a huge thank-you to the editorial team: Jeanenne Ray, Michelle Hacker, Jozette Moses, and (of course) Kirsten Janene-Nelson. Finally, I would like to thank the many leaders I've engaged with over the years. Your courage, drive, and vision inspired me to write this book.

Dr. Brian R. Spisak is a research associate at Harvard's National Preparedness Leadership Initiative. He's also an independent advisor guiding leaders on their digital journey. His passion is helping leaders create opportunities using trailblazing science and technology, well-established leadership research, and invaluable knowledge gleaned from practice. His research is published in top academic journals, and his contributions are featured in popular outlets such as *Harvard Business Review, New Scientist, TIME,* and *The Washington Post.* He's originally from the USA and has since lived in the UK, New Zealand, and the Netherlands.

INDEX

NOTE: Page references in *italics* refer to figures.